The Whistleblowing Guide

The Whistleblowing Guide

Speak-up Arrangements, Challenges, and Best Practices

KATE KENNY
WIM VANDEKERCKHOVE
MARIANNA FOTAKI

WILEY

This edition first published 2019

© 2019 Kate Kenny, Wim Vandekerckhove, and Marianna Fotaki

Registered office

John Wiley & Sons Ltd, The Atrium, Southern Gate, Chichester, West Sussex, PO19 8SQ, United Kingdom

For details of our global editorial offices, for customer services and for information about how to apply for permission to reuse the copyright material in this book please see our website at www.wiley.com.

Wiley publishes in a variety of print and electronic formats and by print-on-demand. Some material included with standard print versions of this book may not be included in e-books or in print-on-demand. If this book refers to media such as a CD or DVD that is not included in the version you purchased, you may download this material at http:// booksupport.wiley.com. For more information about Wiley products, visit www.wiley .com.

Designations used by companies to distinguish their products are often claimed as trademarks. All brand names and product names used in this book are trade names, service marks, trademarks or registered trademarks of their respective owners. The publisher is not associated with any product or vendor mentioned in this book.

Limit of Liability/Disclaimer of Warranty: While the publisher and author have used their best efforts in preparing this book, they make no representations or warranties with respect to the accuracy or completeness of the contents of this book and specifically disclaim any implied warranties of merchantability or fitness for a particular purpose. It is sold on the understanding that the publisher is not engaged in rendering professional services and neither the publisher nor the author shall be liable for damages arising herefrom. If professional advice or other expert assistance is required, the services of a competent professional should be sought.

Library of Congress Cataloging-in-Publication Data

A catalogue record for this book is available from the British Library.

ISBN 978-1-119-36075-9 (hardback) ISBN 978-1-119-36076-6 (ePDF)
ISBN 978-1-119-36078-0 (epub) ISBN 978-1-119-36074-2 (Obook)

Cover Design: Wiley
Cover Image: © BLUR LIFE 1975/Shutterstock

Set in 10/12pt TimesLTStd by SPi Global, Chennai, India

Printed in Great Britain by TJ International Ltd, Padstow, Cornwall, UK

10 9 8 7 6 5 4 3 2 1

Contents

About the Companion Website

This book is accompanied by a companion website:

www.wiley.com/go/Kenny/whistleblowing-guide

The website includes:
- Module Outline
- Presentation
- Cheat Sheet
- Case Studies

CHAPTER 1

Introduction: The Importance of Speak-up Arrangements

SPEAKING UP IN ORGANIZATIONS

Recent years have seen dramatic and fundamental changes in whistleblower procedures for organizations. Prompted by a spate of important public disclosures, organizations are now mandated by law in various countries to implement effective arrangements enabling employees to speak up about perceived wrongdoing. Yet few resources exist to help with this. To fill the gap, this book examines the opportunities and challenges associated with different types of whistleblowing arrangements (often called speak-up systems), and makes recommendations based on best practice. Our proposed model for the effective development of sustainable speak-up systems is rigorously grounded in new, empirical, international research, in a variety of organizational settings along with existing academic literature on the issue.

Whistleblowing forms a key means of addressing dangerous wrongdoing and illegal behaviour in today's organizations. The absence of effective speak-up arrangements prevents organizations and societies from avoiding major disasters. Attempts to alert the authorities to wrongdoing by internal personnel are currently on the increase. However, in many cases, suffering and retaliation experienced by whistleblowers is exacerbated because few if any procedures are in place to receive and follow up on concerns raised by employees. Even when systems are in place, they are often bypassed, and the whistleblower is silenced or over-ruled, as was the case in the Deepwater Horizon oil spill, the collapse of Enron, and the nuclear meltdown after the Fukushima earthquake, for example.[1] Whistleblowing has become an important issue, both for societies, as well as for organizations.

Speak-up arrangements can have economic benefits for organizations and society. They also save money both for private and public sector organizations. A recent study of over 5,000 firms shows that 40% of companies surveyed suffered from serious economic crimes that averaged over $3 million each in losses. Whistleblowers exposed 43% of these crimes, which means that whistleblowing was more effective than all the other measures combined: corporate security, internal audits, and law enforcement.[2] Workers who voice their concern can help to prevent the dysfunctional behaviour that leads to financial and reputational losses by firms and public sector organizations. Ineffective speak-up arrangements, however, limit their ability to do this, and ultimately harm the organization as well as the whistleblower.

The question of how to develop effective speak-up arrangements has become urgent. There is increased media attention for whistleblowers, and policy-makers across the world have lobbied to pass legislation protecting whistleblowers. Although legislation is essential for encouraging speaking up against wrongdoing, it has also drawn our attention to the missing link—that of the organization and its internal arrangements in place for making disclosures. Hence, implementing effective speak-up arrangements is now a vital part of reforming corporate governance, public sector accountability, and professional responsibility. With this book, we hope to contribute to the success of these reforms.

Until now, whistleblowing has mainly been researched from the point of view of the whistleblower. Our research is innovative because it provides insights into speaking-up from the perspective of those who operate the speak-up arrangements.

SPEAK UP ARRANGEMENTS: A NEW PERSPECTIVE FOR THEORY AND PRACTICE

This book offers valuable contributions for academic researchers, professional audiences and managers. It is unique because, unlike other studies and guides, it focuses on the context as well as the organization. We find that these aspects, including legislation cultural norms and economic structures, significantly influence the ways in which speak-up systems are implemented and used 'on the ground'. Our analytic framing allows us to encompass both this 'macro' focus but also a micro-level examination of how such systems are used in the day-to-day activities of those tasked with receiving disclosures.

We find that existing studies of speak-up arrangements are somewhat limited in that they simplify what are, in reality, complex organizational dynamics. The linear, process-oriented models proposed by many scholars fail to capture the fact that speak-up attempts are made in organizational settings in which business-as-usual continues, even when operators are trying to deal with disclosures. Real-life speak-ups rarely if ever progress in a simple fashion: from disclosure, to remedy, to sanction of the wrongdoer. Our research highlights how attempts to achieve each stage are, in practice, made against a backdrop of organizational norms and structures that can represent obstacles to the successful disclosure and resolution of wrongdoing. Moreover, where substantial attempts to remedy a wrongdoing are poorly managed, this can generate paralysis across the organization as an investigation proceeds.

This book also encompasses rich background detail on three important sectors of the economy, currently under the spotlight in the area of speak-up systems not least because of recent scandals: financial services, healthcare and engineering. It includes multinational and national perspectives and examples from both public and private sectors.

Through our analysis of practices across a variety of organizational settings, we offer novel and important insights into commonly misunderstood aspects of internal whistleblowing. We show, for example, how a lack of response, or silence, by the person who receives a disclosure, can be misunderstood by the person speaking up. The person can interpret this as a lack of interest in the wrongdoing, or worse, an indication of their impending marginalization by the organization. This situation is not uncommon. Thus, the onus is on the organization to instill and maintain a culture of responsiveness among managers tasked with receiving speak-ups.

In summary, implementing sustainable speak-up systems in organizations is more complex and intricate than often thought. It involves an intersection of human, technological and organizational dynamics that impact on each other in many ways, through the introduction and use of such arrangements. Radically new perspectives are needed to understand these aspects and to apply them successfully in our organizations. Our research shows how a speak-up arrangement can be implemented successfully. This can be done to ensure retaliation against whistleblowers is minimized, while speak-up operators provide effective and timely feedback to those who raise concerns. Moreover, by showing how speak-up operators attempt to overcome obstacles, we highlight the vital role trust plays for building a culture of openness and transparency in their organizations.

Through the detailed analysis we provide, our study is unusual in that it distills best-practice recommendations by combining both empirical analysis and a detailed review of the relevant literature on the topic, a strategy that enables us to develop a unique and valuable framework by which to understand speak-up arrangements in contemporary organizations.

SUSTAINABLE SPEAK-UP SYSTEMS: A MODEL

This book brings together a variety of perspectives to create a model for the development of sustainable speak-up systems. The key success factors in achieving this are independence, responsiveness, and time. Each of these is explained more fully later in this book.

> *Independence:* The independence of the speak-up recipient is key. Employees are more likely to speak up to a recipient that is removed from the wrongdoing.

Responsiveness: Employees must perceive that their report is being acted on, for speak-up arrangements to work. There are sometimes barriers to how responsive the organization can be.

Time: The preferred channel for speaking up can change with time, as employees get used to the systems that are in place.

To enable independence, to enhance responsiveness, and to support speak-up systems over time, certain contextual features must be present. These are ethical culture and trust.

Ethical culture describes the environment inside an organization that enables and constrains various types of whistleblowing. Kaptein's work in this area for example shows how culture has an impact on how employees speak up, and to whom, whereas Roberts and colleagues show how these dynamics can enhance the success of speak-up systems. As a result of the analysis developed throughout this book, we add trust to this vital aspect. Trust needs to be created in the organization implementing the systems but it must also be maintained over time. For successful speak-ups, whistleblowers and speak-up operators have to make a 'leap of faith' and act on uncertain knowledge. Throughout this book we detail strategies for creating this trust, which include empathy with the whistleblower, and providing a choice of interfaces for the whistleblower to choose from. We also detail strategies for maintaining trust including communications regarding investigations that emerge from speak-ups and the relevant steps, along with operator independence. We describe an important aspect of this framework: the success factors of effective speak-up and the organizational contextual factors that support these are mutually constitutive—this means that the presence of each supports and reinforces the other. In summary, our model of sustainable speak-up systems encompasses the importance of independence, responsiveness and time, and of considering how these intertwine with trust and ethical culture.

RATIONALE

This book is timely. It is vital to study the ways in which whistleblowing/speak-up arrangements are deployed in contemporary organizations, today more than ever, for the following reasons:

- *Changes in legislation.* There has been a significant shift towards encouraging effective speak-up arrangements in organizations. For example, the OECD has published guidelines for protecting whistleblowers,[3] the Council of Europe published recommendations for Europe-wide whistleblower protection,[4] the European Commission proposed a directive to protect individuals that speak up on breaches of EU law.[5] Laws are currently under review in New Zealand and Australia, and several African countries have proposed legislative initiatives.[6]

Industry and sectoral regulators are also increasingly mandating the organizations they regulate to put such measures in place for the internal disclosure of information, and are simultaneously restructuring their own organizations in ways that enable the receipt of information through external disclosures. Internal and external whistleblowing is defined more thoroughly in Chapter 2, but generally refers to disclosing to a member inside the organization or outside the organization respectively. An example comes from the Netherlands; organizations with at least 50 employees are required to have confidential integrity advisors to take disclosures in organizations, although the scope of their role is left intentionally vague,[7] and the House of the Whistleblower has been formed to take external disclosures as well.[8]

From an external perspective, both the FCA and the Care Quality Commission (CQC) in the UK now have dedicated whistleblowing teams registering and following-up whistleblower concerns raised with them. In the United States, a recent Supreme Court judgement has had the effect that whistleblowers are now required to disclose externally to the Securities and Exchange Commission (SEC) to benefit from the protections under the Dodd-Frank Wall Street Reform and Consumer Protection Act (Dodd-Frank) (see Box 1.1). Organizations that wish to encourage internal reporting, then, must have robust disclosure and support systems in place to encourage and facilitate those that wish to speak up. To date, fewer than 30% of organizations have speak-up systems in place, so significant change will be required. Whistleblower protection legislation is currently being drafted at the EU level, for example, guaranteeing that workers in member states will have a minimum level of protection.[9]

BOX 1.1   WHISTLEBLOWING REWARDS IN THE UNITED STATES—*DIGITAL REALTY TRUST INC. V. SOMERS*

In February 2018, the Supreme Court of the United States ruled that protections in the Dodd-Frank Wall Street Reform and Consumer Protection Act 2010 (Dodd- Frank) only applied to whistleblowers who made external disclosures to the Securities and Exchange Commission (SEC). The SEC had previously interpreted the definition of whistleblower widely, allowing those that had made disclosures externally as well as those that had reported internally to avail of the protections under the Dodd-Frank Act. Paul Somers, a manager at Digital Reality Trust, Inc., spoke up to senior managers about his boss hiding millions of dollars in costs that were over the budget, and Somers was fired in 2014. While lower courts agreed with

(Continued)

Somers, the Supreme Court overruled the decision. Whistleblowers in the United States who speak up internally are now only covered by the protections in the Sarbanes-Oxley Act (2002) (SOX). Although SOX still protects whistleblowers against retaliation, they now have a shorter timeframe to bring a lawsuit and are entitled to less compensation than they would be if they brought a case under Dodd-Frank.[10] The Government Accountability Project, the whistleblower advocacy organization in the United States, immediately called for revision in the law saying,

> *For whistleblowers, it strips Dodd Frank legal protection against retaliation for the 96 percent of corporate whistleblowers who never break company ranks. For corporations, it forces employees to go behind the company's back and run to the government whenever they see internal misconduct. Otherwise there will be no legal rights. For the SEC, it will mean a tidal wave of new investigative work if employees can no longer safely work through corporate ranks to challenge illegality. Congress never intended this result, and must act quickly to clarify poorly written statutory language. Otherwise corporate dysfunction will replace corporate accountability.[11]*

- *Whistleblowing forms a key means of addressing dangerous wrongdoing and dysfunctional behaviour in today's organizations.* The absence of effective speak-up arrangements prevents organizations and societies from avoiding major disasters.[12] For this reason, whistleblowing has become an important issue, both for societies as well as for organizations. Attempts to alert the authorities to wrongdoing by internal personnel are currently increasing. In healthcare for example, whistleblowing to the media led to the Public Inquiry into the Mid-Staffordshire Hospital Trust, and an enduring stream of NHS whistleblower cases triggered the *Freedom to Speak Up Review.*[13] In Ireland, the treatment and attempted silencing of a whistleblower in An Garda Síochána (the Irish police force) led to the Charleton tribunal, which is still ongoing at the time of writing. In the wake of the financial crisis, in the United States the Securities and Exchange Commission (SEC) received 3,620 cases through whistleblower disclosures in the fiscal year 2014, up 10% from 2013, and 21% compared to 2012,[14] and the Occupational Safety and Health Administration (OSHA) shows a generally increasing trend from 2007 to the present.[15] In the UK, reports to the Financial Conduct Authority (FCA) have increased significantly over the past few years.[16]

- *Ineffective speak-up arrangements lead to suffering by whistleblowers.* Over 30 years of research shows us that although the logic of democratic institutions is dependent upon courageous individuals speaking up to publicize wrongdoing[17] such individuals are often, paradoxically, ostracized and retaliated against for disclosures that aim to counteract corruption and protect the public interest.[18] In many cases, suffering and retaliation were exacerbated because few if any procedures were in place to facilitate disclosure. Speak-up arrangements must focus on protecting the individual, as a first priority, and in-depth research is required to determine best practice for developing effective processes and structures.
- *Effective speak-up arrangements have economic benefits for organizations and society.* Whistleblowing is important from a societal and an ethical perspective, but it also saves money both for private and public sector organizations. Such disclosures can help to prevent the illegal behaviour that leads to financial and reputational losses by firms and public sector organizations.[19] As mentioned earlier, whistleblowers exposed economic crimes that averaged over $3 million in losses for companies that corporate security, internal audit and law enforcement were not able to detect.[20] The absence of effective measures means that organizations and institutions are denied an opportunity to address the wrongdoing that whistleblowers perceive, early on in the process, and thus lose time, money and effort by having to engage in protracted and unnecessary legal battles.

WHO SHOULD READ THIS BOOK?

- *Managers in contemporary organizations who must implement speak-up arrangements.* The book is a practical resource for use by managers who implement speak-up procedures because it offers advice on creating effective procedures for speaking up when wrongdoing is observed. This advice is also useful for managers who are seeking to enhance existing speak-up arrangements. It will also appeal to policy-makers internationally who despite actively advocating the use of speak-up arrangements have little empirical research upon which to draw. Readers from these groups will learn about effective procedures that enable whistleblowers to remain protected while disclosing information and explaining how to militate against the kinds of retaliations previously experienced by this group. Other readers include regulators who encourage such changes, professional bodies who advise their members on implementing and using speak-up arrangements, trade unions and other organizations who play a role in conflict mediation, and academics.
- *Organizations that regularly engage with whistleblowers.* Readers from these groups will learn how to offer evidence-based advice on how to effectively raise concerns through speak-up arrangements, making whistleblowers able

to more effectively disclose information to both organizations internally and regulators if needed.

- *Policy-makers, public representatives, and professional bodies involved in whistleblower procedures.* This group includes Parliamentary Select Committees, 'prescribed persons' under country-specific legislation, including regulators, and professional bodies along with the advocacy groups that are actively engaging with organizations to implement speak-up arrangements, for example. These readers will become better informed about this key issue, which will help them make appropriate decisions about how to best to support whistleblowers and how to advise organizations.

- *Academics.* This book integrates conceptual work on the nature of speak-up arrangements and the factors that contribute to their effectiveness, including the theoretical framework outlined earlier. Currently, little is known about the complex factors that enhance effective speak-up arrangements. Deeper understanding is required to enhance knowledge in this area and inform policy debates. This book is a first step in this direction and academic readers will learn the basics of speak-up arrangements so they can build on it with future research.

PURPOSE OF THE BOOK

After reading this book, readers will be able to:

1. **Identify the major organizational, structural, and cultural obstacles to speaking up through speak-up arrangements, in their own organizations.** As detailed in this book, obstacles include employees' lack of awareness about such procedures, a lack of training and experience in how to use the internal/external procedures, expectations of inaction from previous experiences, and middle managers' risk aversion in effectively addressing issues, despite being the first recipients of whistleblower concerns.

2. **Propose effective whistleblowing and speak-up arrangements in their organizations.** This involves an understanding of the significance of culture, power, responsiveness, and trust in the implementation and use of a successful speak-up procedure, along with the organizational changes required to design and implement these.

3. **Understand the specific policy and legislation requirements that can promote or impede the effective implementation of speak-up arrangements,** and how these can be translated into commercial and public organizations across sectors and cultures.

4. **Distinguish between internal and external reporting arrangements**. The book offers information and clarification on key issues, including the distinction between internal and external speak-up procedures, which is in practice somewhat blurred.

ABOUT THE AUTHORS

The book benefits from the significant experience of its three authors in the area of whistleblowing research, in the public sector (Vandekerckhove), health and social care (Fotaki), and banking and financial services (Kenny). All authors have significant expertise in researching and writing about the topic of whistleblowing and speaking out: Kate Kenny carried out an in-depth study into whistleblowing in banking and finance organizations in the UK, Ireland, Switzerland, and the United States, with a focus on compliance and risk officers.[21] She has assisted *Public Concern at Work (now Protect)*, the *Financial Conduct Authority* and *Transparency International Ireland* on their whistleblowing research and communications. Her publications draw on critical and psychosocial theories to develop new perspectives on whistleblowing.[22] Her recent collaborative work focuses on postdisclosure survival strategies of whistleblowers across a variety of sectors. Wim Vandekerckhove was the lead in a qualitative research study on the implementation of whistleblowing arrangements in the NHS for the Freedom to Speak Up Review,[23] and carried out research on Belgian public and private sector whistleblowing arrangements for a Transparency International country report on Belgium.[24] He has also collaborated with *Public Concern at Work (now Protect)* on the analysis of 1,000 cases from their whistleblower helpline.[25] He has provided expertise to the Council of Europe, the Dutch Whistleblower Authority, and Transparency International on a number of occasions as well. He is currently involved in committees developing a whistleblowing standard with the British Standards Institute and the International Organization for Standardization (ISO). Marianna Fotaki has worked on the role of internal auditors as internal whistleblowers in government agencies in Indonesia, with an internal auditor seconded into the project funded by the World Bank.[26] She has also worked as the EU advisor for governments of Russia, Armenia, and Georgia on governance of Social Security, health, and public policy for 10 years in total. Fotaki has been involved in various projects on the impact of introducing market incentives on the quality of healthcare systems in the NHS in England and how the pressure to produce savings by management affects health staff's behaviour leading to widespread patient abuse and the systematic perversion of care.[27] More recently, she advised the United Nations Office on Drugs and Crime and helped developing ethics modules for the Education for Justice (E4J) initiative.[28] Marianna is a member of the Academic Board of Academy of Business in Society (ABIS) and co-directs pro-bono with the Centre for Health and the Public Interest. She is also involved with the European Business Ethics Network (EBEN).

In addition to research focus, each author brings academic expertise:

Vandekerckhove brings expertise in comparative studies of the institutional dimensions of whistleblowing procedures and legislation; Fotaki brings expertise in health with a focus on mental health, psychoanalytic, and psychosocial approaches, along with a specific focus on business ethics and public governance. This complements Kenny's expertise on whistleblowing and organizational culture and identity, with a focus on the banking and finance sector, all of which are essential for the purpose of this project. We have and continue to work with key organizations in this area: the Government Accountability Project (US), Transparency International (Ireland, Belgium and Berlin) and Whistleblowers UK.

Finally we would like to thank Research Assistants Meghan Van Portfliet and Didem Derya Ozdemir for their invaluable help on this project.'

ABOUT THE BOOK

Chapter 2 begins with a discussion of how law-makers and organizations are increasingly requiring that speak-up arrangements be implemented, and what implications this has for whistleblowers where there is no encouragement or support for them to speak up, highlighting retaliation as one of the possible consequences. We then consider the existing literature and use it to debunk several myths. We show that whistleblowing is a process and not a one-off event by presenting data that shows whistleblowers make multiple disclosures to increasingly independent recipients. Additionally, we show that internal and external whistleblowing are not separate occurrences, but are usually part of the same process.

Next, we introduce some theoretical ideas from the literature: we examine the research on employee voice because whistleblowing can be understood as an act of employees using this capacity in their organizations to speak up about wrongdoings. We debunk the traditional myths from several research streams and show how the focus on motivation for speaking up is less important than the fact that it happens in organizations. This act of speaking up has been researched using the concept of fearless speech (parrhesia), which we also examine to describe and highlight the importance of the hearer of speak-ups. We then link this fearless speech to concepts of trust: between the employee and the organization, and in interpersonal connections. We next examine empirical research that has been carried out in organizations that have implemented speak-up systems and note some key findings including the importance of an internal champion for the initiative to succeed.

Chapter 3 draws on existing literature and primary research carried out by the authors (which was generously funded by ACCA and ESRC) to present three case studies of whistleblowing in the finance, engineering, and health sectors. A full outline of the study's methods is given in the Appendix. This research is important because there are few empirical studies into this topic.[29] The case studies are based on research that was conducted in different organizational and geographical cultural settings. These include (1) implementing speak-up arrangements at an NHS Trust (UK, public sector); (2) implementing speak-up arrangements at an engineering multinational firm (UK and multiple continents, private sector); and (3) implementing speak-up arrangements at a leading retail bank (UK and Ireland, private sector).

The chapter starts with a discussion of the banking sector, illustrating the pervasiveness of a culture of silence that exists in such organizations. Reasons for this silence are identified, which include failure to investigate claims, retaliation against voicing employees and social isolation of voicing employees from colleagues. Next the engineering sector is featured, highlighting the serious consequences that can result from wrongdoing in this area, and the ethical codes that have been implemented. Finally, the healthcare sector is examined with a focus on the NHS in the UK. The issues that have arisen from the decision to run the institution according to market principles are discussed. Case studies are presented for each sector, and key learnings are discussed. To conclude the chapter, parallels and differences in speak-up mechanisms and culture across sectors are pointed out, and the economic and political context that informs the culture is discussed.

Chapter 4 begins with an overview of Kaptein's research on how culture influences the decision to speak up or not, and then revisits speaking up as a protracted process in more detail, building on the discussion from Chapter 2. Next, we discuss the expectations that are intertwined with speaking up, drawing on Watzlawick's communication theory and Bird's idea of 'muted conscience'. We then present some of the challenges to operating speak-up channels, highlighting the concepts of independence, responsiveness and time, and drawing on our own research for examples of these challenges in practice. Following this, we consider some of the barriers to responsiveness and the role trust plays in facilitating responsive behaviour. Finally, we conclude with recommendations on how to use the speak-up data that is captured when arrangements are in place to help assess the receptiveness of an organization towards employee voice.

The overall aim of the book is to provide a practical guide that is strongly informed by critical interpretation of the relevant research including our own and other academic work. By drawing on various empirical and theoretical frames, we are able to present whistleblowing as a collective endeavour, show the importance of mutual support of employees who wish to speak up, as well as the necessity of fostering a culture of openness and transparency that is conducive to promoting fearless speech. All of these ideas can be used by managers to implement speak-up arrangements that are effective and protect both whistleblowers and the organization. We begin in Chapter 2 by discussing the importance of speak-up arrangements.

ENDNOTES

1. Ionescu (2015: 57); Kenny (2019); Kenny, Fotaki, and Scriver (2018).
2. Devine (2012).
3. OECD (2011).
4. Council of Europe (2014).
5. EU Commission (2018).

6. Blueprint for Free Speech (2018).
7. De Graaf (2016).
8. Boone (2016); van Steenbergen (2014).
9. Rankin (2018); EU Commission (2018).
10. Gresko (2018).
11. Government Accountability Project (2018).
12. Devine and Maassarani (2011).
13. Francis (2015).
14. SEC (2014).
15. OSHA (2018).
16. FCA (2015a).
17. For example, see Berwick (2013); Harding (2014); O'Brien (2003).
18. Alford (2001); Devine and Maassarani (2011).
19. Roberts et al. (2011).
20. Devine (2012).
21. Kenny (2014); Kenny (2018).
22. Kenny (2017); Kenny, Fotaki, and Scriver (2018); Kenny, Fotaki, and Vandekerckhove (2019); Kenny (2019); Vandekerckhove, Fotaki, Kenny, Humantito, and Ozdemir Kaya (2016).
23. Vandekerckhove and Rumyantseva (2014).
24. Vandekerckhove (2013).
25. Vandekerckhove (2013).
26. Fotaki and Humantito (2015).
27. Francis (2013).
28. See https://www.unodc.org/dohadeclaration/en/topics/education-for-justice.html for more information on this project.
29. Miceli, Near, and Dworkin (2008).

CHAPTER 2

Why Speak-up Systems: Why Now?

INTRODUCTION

Speak-up arrangements is the term currently used for internal whistleblowing procedures. The phrase represents an attempt to avoid the negative connotations of the term 'whistleblowing' as denoting a squealer or snitch.[1] Whistleblowing is 'the disclosure by organization members (former or current) of illegal, immoral, or illegitimate practices under the control of their employers, to persons or organizations that may be able to effect action'.[2] Whistleblowing as a term has been in use since the 1970s, and it has been the subject of much research. Topics range from whether instances of whistleblowing can be accurately predicted in a given organizational setting,[3] to legal frameworks protecting whistleblowers' rights and the impacts of retaliation by organizations on those who speak up.

This book focuses on how best to facilitate whistleblowing within organizations in a safe and effective manner, such that first, the wrongdoing that has been identified can be rectified and second, and equally important, the person raising the alarm can be protected. This is an area of growing concern both in academic literature[4] and in professional practice. Encouraging people to speak up about perceived wrongdoing is not easy, particularly in organizational cultures in which silence is the norm, and where there is little support available for speaking out.[5] Given the importance of whistleblowers for society and for organizations as described in Chapter 1, it is vital to pursue this field of study.

BACKGROUND: WHY SPEAK-UP SYSTEMS, WHY NOW?

A shift towards encouraging effective speak-up arrangements in organizations has been visible lately in the activities of key actors across a range of institutional settings.

From an external perspective, that is, for whistleblowers going outside of their organization to report wrongdoing*, industry and sectoral regulators are increasingly restructuring their own processes such that they are able to receive information passed on through external disclosures. For example, in the UK, both the FCA and the Care Quality Commission (CQC) now have dedicated whistleblowing teams registering and following-up whistleblower concerns raised with them. At the internal level in organizations, many guidelines for organizational whistleblowing policy have recently been developed.[6] These emerge in response to an increase in legislative protection for whistleblowers in a number of countries,[7] as well as to regulators who signal that organizations are responsible for creating cultures that encourage internal whistleblowing. Indeed, many now insist that the organizations they regulate implement robust measures for the internal disclosure of information.[8] In the context of the UK financial sector for example, in their recent joint consultation paper, the Prudential Regulation Authority (PRA) and the Financial Conduct Authority (FCA)[9] discussed the option of sanctioning organizations that lack or operate inadequate internal whistleblowing arrangements. Indeed, the FCA now obliges all deposit-holding institutions to have a 'champion' in place: a dedicated senior person to deal with internal whistleblowing reports. Organizations will be fined if they do not have such policies. In the UK health sector, the Freedom to Speak Up Review (Francis Report) was published in 2015 following a detailed inquiry in 2013. Its focus was the failings in care provision within an NHS Foundation Trust. The review notes the requirement for all NHS trusts to alter their structures such that a specified individual would act as a 'whistleblower guardian', who would oversee whistleblowing procedures and arrangements from within the organization.[10]

Such changes are not without consequence, however, and give rise to new issues. For example, it is likely that these organizational whistleblowing procedures and arrangements will now also have to pass scrutiny of external audit and satisfy an externally defined standard, such as the UK Code of Practice suggested by Public Concern at Work,[11] and taken over by the Department for Business, Innovation and Skills (BIS) in its guidance to employers.[12] This shift necessarily increases the demands placed on internal audit, as it is likely that this will result in an increased accountability for internal auditors with regard to effective speak-up arrangements. In addition these changes take place against a legal backdrop that is frequently shifting. (See Box 1.1.)

As with all significant changes in organizational cultures and structures, the implementation of speak-up arrangements will have wide and far-reaching

---

*See section on internal and external whistleblowing later in this chapter.

implications and thus must be treated seriously by the organizations involved. The insights developed in this chapter leads us to conclude by proposing a new approach to this key issue.

Importance of Effective Speak-up Systems: The Issue of Retaliation

Where there is little or no effective support available within organizations for speaking up about risky, illegal or dangerous activities, people who do so can be at risk of retaliation. Organizational retaliation is unfortunately a common response to whistleblowing,[13] and it appears to be increasing.[14] Rehg et al. define it as undesirable action taken against a whistleblower—in direct response to the whistle-blowing (sic)—who reported wrongdoing internally or externally, outside the organization.[15] Reasons for retaliation vary; managers can feel deeply threatened by whistleblowers,[16] whereas both employers and co-workers can resort to reprisals to protect the reputation of specific colleagues[17] or the organization itself.[18] Thus, retaliation can come from a variety of sources.[19]

Retaliation can also be deployed as a means of deterring other potential whistleblowers in the organization,[20] for example in the case of Jeffery Wigand at Brown & Williamson Tobacco Corp.[21] Jeffrey Wigand was hired as a scientist for a tobacco company in 1989. During the time he was employed, he witnessed various wrongdoing, from the changing of minutes to remove incriminating information, to the smuggling of seeds in cigarette boxes, and the cover up of the dangers of cigarettes. He reported his concerns to his boss, and was subsequently fired. Later, after hearing a tobacco executive lie under oath about the harmful effects of tobacco, he took his story to the media. He was then told by a Kentucky judge that he would be jailed if he spoke about tobacco matters. This treatment was in part a desperate attempt by the tobacco industry to discourage others who had the same information from speaking out.[22]

When retaliation is used to silence not only the whistleblower but others who could potentially speak out, it represents a 'disciplinary' form of power—that is, where transgressions of tacit organizational norms are publicly reprimanded so as to discourage others. For Alford[23] this works through the 'language of science and medicine', or how we use ideas from these fields to describe organizations as 'organisms' or something whole and objectively definable. Whistleblowers are therefore a threat, 'infecting' the organization; something that needs to be purged. The result is twofold—the isolating of whistleblowers such that both their behaviour and their personalities become subject to scrutiny, and casting them as suspect 'outsiders' who represent a threat to the organization.

BOX 2.1   EILEEN FOSTER AND COUNTRYWIDE BANK

Eileen Foster started working for Countrywide Bank in 2005 as a vice president, and by 2007 she had been promoted to executive vice president of Fraud Risk Management. It was in summer of 2007, in this senior role, that she was tipped off by an employee in one of the regional offices that dealt with subprime loans. He informed Foster's team that there was fraud occurring in the office, that employees were altering or forging documents with the result that customers were being signed up to loans they could not afford, and were not qualified to take out. He explained that he had tried to report it but was fired for doing so. Foster had some of her group investigate this branch and discovered that the allegation was true.[24]

By the beginning of 2008, Foster's team had uncovered similar fraudulent activities in Miami, Chicago, Cincinnati, San Diego, Las Vegas and Los Angeles.[25] *Foster began to suspect that employee relations and lending managers were colluding to hide the fraud. Employees that reported the wrongdoing were transferred, harassed or terminated, but the managers that were in charge of these branches were merely transferred to other roles. Foster decided to report the issues to internal audit, asking that they investigate the employee relations team. Internal audit, however, did not look into employee relations but started investigating Foster. They interviewed her staff, in one case keeping a colleague for almost three hours, aggressively questioning him in a style that appeared designed to prompt him to say negative things about Foster.*

In the meantime, Bank of America acquired Countrywide. Foster was promoted and so began to hope that things would change. Her hopes were dashed, however, when she was presented with a deal for almost $230,000 in return for her silence about what she had seen. She refused to sign and was then fired in September 2008 for her 'inappropriate and unprofessional behaviour' and 'poor judgment as a leader'.

Foster, however, decided to keep fighting, and filed a Sarbanes-Oxley Act whistleblower complaint with OSHA, claiming her termination was illegal. In September 2011, OSHA ruled that Foster had been retaliated against in violation of the employee protection provision of the Sarbanes Oxley Corporate and Criminal Fraud Accountability Act of 2002. The Department of Labor ordered her reinstatement and $930,000 in damages. Foster was also awarded the Ridenhour Prize for truthtelling in 2012.

(Adapted from Government Accountability Project, 2012)

Retaliation can take a number of forms[26] including demotion, decreased quality of working conditions,[27] threats by senior staff, the allocation of menial duties to the whistleblower such that their job becomes degrading, harassment, referral to psychiatrists,[28] outright dismissal from work and prolonged legal challenges (see Box 2.1). Retaliation can also include tactics aimed at stigmatizing the individual for example through character assassinations or accusations of being disgruntled employees, spies, or 'squealers',[29] which are sometimes upheld by the media.[30] These tactics are supported by ambivalent perceptions of whistleblowing in wider society; it is often seen as a 'morally ambiguous activity'.[31] Although some view it as heroic,[32] others see whistleblowing as a traitorous violation of loyalty to one's organization.[33] However, ambivalence could also mean that the general public may not care enough to do anything to support the whistleblower, or oppose the mistreatment of those that speak up.

We know that retaliation is stronger where the person has disclosed information about systemic and deep-seated wrongdoing as opposed to isolated incidents,[34] and retaliation also increases where the whistleblower has gone outside of the organization to report—for example, to an external regulator or journalist.[35] This all means that whistleblowing can have disproportionately severe implications for those who engage in it, where adequate protections are not in place. A person's quality of life and health can suffer badly;[36] whistleblowers struggle to find work in their industry[37] and this can exacerbate the impacts of the whistleblowing process, which include financial difficulties, and problems with physical health.[38] Whistleblowers are often 'treated as disturbed or morally suspect'.[39] Because of this negative perception and a general reluctance by the general public to do anything to counteract negativity, retaliatory tactics have impacts on whistleblowers' mental health including depression, anxiety, feelings of isolation and symptoms analogous to post-traumatic stress,[40] along with sleep difficulties[41] and in some cases suicidal feelings[42] despite that, prior to their disclosures, many were 'high-achieving, respected' and committed employees.[43]

BOX 2.2   LENNANE'S PIONEERING RESEARCH ON RETALIATION AND THE ROLE OF THE ORGANIZATION

Jean Lennane, a whistleblower and a psychiatrist, and also a former president of Whistleblowers Australia, conducted a survey of 35 whistleblowers in Australia to understand what happens to them and why. The results showed the lengths to which the organizations went to silence individuals that spoke up about corruption. The reprisals taken were swift, and coordinated throughout the organizations, and whistleblowers were left with

(Continued)

symptoms that last years after the speak-up is made. Symptoms reported include panic attacks, trouble sleeping, loss of confidence, depression, suicidal thoughts, feelings of guilt and unworthiness, loss of weight, high blood pressure, and others.

Informal Reprisals	% Affected
Isolation from information	49
Physical isolation from other staff	23
Removal of normal work	43
Abuse and denigration (usually by supervisor)	43
Minute scrutiny of time sheets and other work records	34
Impossible orders	26
Referral for psychiatric assessment	20

Formal Reprisal	% Affected
Dismissed from job	20
Demoted	14
Transferred to another town	14
Pressured to Resign	43
Position Abolished	9

Lenanne highlights that the role of the organization is key, because it has the resources and the power to either solve the problem or silence the whistleblower. She writes: 'It is exceedingly difficult, even when both sides want a matter settled, to achieve it expeditiously. When one side does not want it settled, or indeed to get into open court, and that side has the power and money, it can be drawn out almost indefinitely, for as long as necessary to exhaust the whistleblower's emotional and financial resources'.[44]

In her pioneering work surveying postdisclosure experiences of 35 individuals who contacted Whistleblowers Australia, Jeanne Lennane reports on the causes of such issues, including being removed from normal work duties or required to fulfil overly demanding tasks, being isolated from colleagues and/or referral to a psychiatrist, while the stress accompanying whistleblowing can cause people to lose their livelihood and to experience marital breakdown, substance abuse and bankruptcy not least from expensive lawsuits[45] (see Box 2.2). Even when not referred by their organizations, many whistleblowers require psychiatric counselling to help them cope with the process.[46] Adding to these problems, mental illness is itself highly stigmatized,[47] which can result in discrediting of the individual identified as mentally ill (see Box 2.3).

BOX 2.3   MENTAL HEALTH AND WHISTLEBLOWING

In their research on mental health and whistleblowing, Kenny, Fotaki, and Scriver[48] find that both organizations and whistleblowers use the concept of 'mental health' in different ways. Organizations, when retaliating against whistleblowers often send them for psychiatric evaluation, with the aim of showing that the whistleblower is not mentally stable and therefore not someone to be trusted. Because mental health is a stigmatized concept in society, questioning this aspect of the whistleblower undermines them and delegitimizes their claim by calling their character into question. To combat this, whistleblowers have to put aside all emotion when dealing with the organization, not showing anger, frustration or any other sentiment that will legitimate the organization's claim that they are affected mentally.

Outside the organization, however, whistleblowers can use the concept of mental health to their advantage. Often, to deal with the stress, isolation and retaliation, whistleblowers do seek out counselling. In court cases this can be used to assert that the whistleblower has suffered in their mental and emotional well-being at the hands of the organization. When the whistleblowers deploy the concept, the intention is not to undermine their claim, but rather showcase the extreme malfeasance of the organization in how they responded to and treated the whistleblower.

Mental health then is a concept that can be used by either side in a whistleblowing struggle to gain power and advantage, and it is an example of how even though power is thought to be concentrated on the side of the organization in whistleblowing cases, it can instead be seen as dynamic, moving among actors.

Additionally, in their earlier research examining whistleblower identity from different sectors and countries, Fotaki, Kenny and Scriver[49] found that can experience multiple instances of stress, anxiety and fear before and during the whistleblowing process. At the same time, the active retaliations very often deployed by organizations causes whistleblowers to suffer from a variety of mental conditions that can be used against them to delegitimize their disclosures. Hence, mental health struggles are a pervasive feature

(Continued)

of some whistleblowers' stories and this can radically reduce the person's likelihood of success. The whistleblower is more likely to simply give in, the more oppressive the struggle with mental well-being. In addition, mental health issues can be actively suppressed by the whistleblower, thus taking them off the table and out of sight. For a wrongdoer company planning a strategy of discrediting, this often provides an opportunity to escalate its retaliatory tactics. The mental health of litigants can be used by organizations in defending allegations of retaliation—for example, stating that the claimant was mentally ill and not acting in the public interest, and/or in good faith. This can result in diverting attention away from the seriousness of disclosure, exonerating the organization from any criticism of these impacts on the person. Finally, organizations can in some cases use information about psychiatric assistance and other related issues, to further demean the person making the claims.

Retaliation can have devastating effects on the whistleblower but also, it can ensure that the original wrongdoing that was the source of the disclosure, remains unchecked. This is because as Martin and Rifkin note, whistleblowing retaliation is not a simple interaction but rather can involve an ever-increasing spiral of resentment on both sides, as each successive interaction leads to more entrenched positions.[50] On the one hand the whistleblower grows ever more determined to see their disclosures are heard and also to ensure justice for the wrongdoing, while, on the other hand, the organization resolves to destroy the source of trouble. For these reasons among others, it is vital that proposed speak-up systems would aim in the first instance to minimize the impact of speaking up on the person disclosing the information.

Existing Research into Speak-up Arrangements in Organizations

Although it is clearly an important issue, the question of how to develop procedures that are both safe and effective has not received great attention from academic researchers. Thus far, debates around whistleblowing have, in general, focused largely on whistleblowing legislation,[51] not least because of recent pushes by policy-makers across the world to pass laws protecting whistleblowers as part of reforming corporate governance, public sector accountability and professional responsibility.[52] Although legislation is essential for encouraging speaking up against wrongdoing, such a focus within academic debates means that a key level is missed: that of the organization, the arrangements in place for speaking up and the development and maintenance of a culture that facilitates their effective use. This contributes to a major gap in how these systems are implemented: we know little about how this can best be done. Although the legislation protecting whistleblowers from retaliation by their employers that exists in many countries is essential, without effective internal and external measures, adequate structures and supportive cultures for reporting wrongdoing, success is unlikely. Reporting and correcting wrongdoing is key to establishing an ethical culture, and having structures in place helps encourage employees to speak up about the wrongdoing that they may witness.[53] Policy must therefore be linked to organizational analysis and understanding. Moreover, by failing to do this, a valuable opportunity is being missed: research shows that having whistleblowing procedures in place in an organization can in fact foster more ethical behaviour.[54]

Another popular strand of literature focuses on the individual whistleblower.[55] Studies in this vein look at motivations of whistleblowers, and also what happens to them postdisclosure. Although useful, it again misses the practical need to study how such individuals might be supported at the early stage. In short, there is limited research focusing specifically on issues pertaining to the implementation of speak-up arrangements, and from the perspective of those responsible. In what follows, we first challenge some common myths in relation to whistleblowing in order to paint a clearer picture of speaking up in organizations and what it involves, before moving later in the chapter to more specific research on the topic of whistleblowing arrangements in organizations.

Revisiting the Myths

Whistleblowing as Process, Not Event Although it is commonly believed that blowing the whistle is a one-off event, involving a single act of disclosure, in reality it involves an ongoing process.[56] Whistleblowing as a protracted process is discussed in more depth in Chapter 4, but a brief introduction to this view helps put the research in context. Whilst the act of whistleblowing is the moment at which information is disclosed, the whistleblowing process, the complex and sometimes lengthy events that both lead up to and emerge after the disclosure, must be incorporated into any understanding of what whistleblowing is. Whistleblowing as a process inherently involves multiple actors: the wrongdoer, the whistleblower, and various real and potential recipients of the information (see Box 2.4). Whistleblowers try to raise their concern more than once,[57] most often first with the wrongdoer directly or with their line manager. When this is not successful they then tend to either turn to someone else within the organization or seek an external recipient (a regulator or the media). It often takes a number of attempts to raise a concern before the disclosed information is investigated. This investigation also takes time.

BOX 2.4   WHISTLEBLOWING AS A PROTRACTED PROCESS

Although historically whistleblowing has been thought of as a single event (an employee speaking up once to a recipient) Vandekerckhove and Phillips found in a study of 1000 UK whistleblowing cases that whistleblowing is a process rather than a single event.[58] Whistleblowers often made more than one disclosure, and reported internally two or even three times before reporting externally, if they went externally at all. This view of speaking up as a protracted, or drawn out, process sheds light on a number of assumptions that existed in the literature before.

First whistleblowers generally follow the hierarchy when reporting: who they report to depends on who they reported to previously. If a manager doesn't fix the issue, whistleblowers will go to higher management or a specialist channel, for example. Previous research did not distinguish between multiple internal attempts and assumed that whistleblowers disclosed externally if internal channels didn't work. Although this is true in a sense, it overlooks that whistleblowers try several times to disclose to different internal recipients, and that the whistleblower seeks increasingly independent respondents to hear their concerns. An example of this can be seen in the case of Maurice McCabe, a whistleblower in An Garda Síochána, the police force in in Ireland. McCabe disclosed wrongdoing to his superior officers, the superintendent of his territory, the comptroller and auditor general and to the Minister of Justice before going outside the formal channels and testifying to the Public Accounts Committee.

Second, the formal power of whistleblowers was previously thought to influence how effective they are at speaking up. This study finds that whistleblowers in higher, more skilled positions start out differently than those in a lower or unskilled level, but that as the process goes on, the results end up the same for both groups in terms of what happens to them. All whistleblowers suffer more, the longer the whistleblowing process is, as the chance of retaliation and dismissal increases at each attempt to speak up. An example of this is Eileen Foster (see Box 2.1). She was a senior executive and had significant formal power, but each time she spoke up, she was subjected to more and more retaliation until she was eventually fired.

Finally, this study shows that whistleblowers try to fix the problem internally multiple times first, even though whistleblowing can be more effective when external bodies get involved and the organization is not in control of whether concern is considered to be legitimate or not. In the cases studied, 80% of all disclosures (including second, third and fourth attempts) were internal, 16% were external and approximately 3% were to the union.

Although the number of those making external disclosures increases as the process becomes more protracted, it never exceeds the quantity making internal disclosures.

This is important for managers, as they are more often than not the last ones who can do something about the disclosure and protect the whistle-blower.

As research on whistleblowing continues, myths around the topic that have emerged can be evaluated and confirmed, or dispelled (see Box 2.5). One such myth that has been dismissed is that whistleblowing is a one-off event. Rather, speaking up is a process where the whistleblower discloses information to a series of people until the issue is resolved. When implementing speak-up arrangements, then, it is important to understand how a whistleblower approaches this process, and to design it accordingly, with multiple internal channels that are increasingly more independent so the whistleblower has options before going external to the organization. More on this internal/external distinction is discussed next.

BOX 2.5   OTHER COMMON MYTHS ABOUT WHISTLEBLOWING SYSTEMS

Opting out of providing robust whistleblowing systems is no longer an option. Many organizations still have no such systems. Those that do frequently report that they are not effective.

Whistleblowing is seldom out of the news these days, with scandals in some of Ireland's most well-known organizations. Whistleblowing is not just a news story, though: it is a serious matter for any senior manager in Ireland. Recent legislation—the Protected Disclosures Act 2014—has changed the game. It increases protection for people who speak up about perceived wrongdoing. It also means that employers who fail to have robust whistleblowing systems risk prosecution for failing to take whistleblowing seriously, for failing to ensure anonymity for people and for not protecting their whistleblowing employees. Opting out of providing robust whistleblowing systems is no longer an option.

A significant gap exists. Many organizations still have no such systems. Those that do frequently report that they are not effective. Many organizations don't train their staff in how to use such protocols. This amounts to

(Continued)

a dangerous "box-ticking" approach to whistleblowing systems. It leaves employers vulnerable.

Employees are even more at risk and are aware of this. Research shows that more than 50% of managers would prefer not speak up about wrong-doing, out of concern for their reputation and career prospects. Much needs to be done if speak-up systems are to be effective.

When we carried out our research into "best practice" in whistleblow-ing systems, which we detail throughout, we encountered three common myths.

Myth one: Encouraging disclosures is enough.

Speak-up systems succeed or fail based on whether they are trusted. But the nature of disclosure means it is difficult for even the most well-meaning employer to build this trust. When someone makes a disclosure, they are waiting for signals that they have been taken seriously and their claim acted upon. However, because of legal limits, employers are often prevented from sharing results of investigations. And if the disclosure was anonymous, the organization has no way to contact the person who made it. Finally, if sanc-tions against an individual wrongdoer have been taken as a result of a dis-closure, including a reprimand or a formal warning, these may not be visible to the discloser. Limited or no feedback can leave the disclosing employee feeling worried that their concern was not taken seriously. They can men-tion concerns to colleagues and the speak-up system may then be perceived as not working.

What can companies or organizations do? They need to ensure they are communicating with absolute clarity on the next steps following a disclosure—what will happen and what feedback, if any, is possible.

Myth two: Senior management will be trusted to receive disclosures.

Implementing even the most sophisticated system is no guarantee that they will be used. A recent study showed that fewer than 40% of employ-ees feel their senior managers support whistleblowing. Strategies for build-ing trust through being as responsive as possible, described earlier, are just not enough. First, where the whistleblowing system is "housed" needs to be carefully considered. This can set the tone for whether it is trusted. For example, the bank we researched initially managed the process through its compliance department. However, employees perceived that group to have more of a "policing" function. That prompted the bank to rehouse the whistleblowing structure within human resources. Here it was seen as a sys-tem that ostensibly put the employee's well-being first. Second, offering an independent channel as part of the speak-up policy is essential. This could involve an external advice organization that has no contractual obligation to report back to one's senior management. Best practice is to offer this as part of a suite of options. Third, clarity around anonymity and confidentiality is absolutely key, because this represents one of the major barriers to people coming forward. Finally, without the visible and sustained support of senior management, implementations of speak-up systems are likely to fail. Surprisingly, the more successful organizations do not ignore "irrelevant" disclosures, including those related to grievances or other minor matters. Rather these are used as opportunities to showcase responsiveness and build trust. The questions, the answers, and clarity around whether they qualified as disclosures are shared with all employees.

Myth three: Implementing robust speak-up systems will "solve" corruption.

Encouraging people to come forward takes a lot of time and care, because it requires a genuine change in culture to build the trust required. In one multinational engineering firm, managers reported that it took 10 years after the initial system was implemented for a culture to emerge in which most people trusted management sufficiently to come forward. It takes time.[59]

Internal and External Whistleblowing: Not an "Either/Or" When a person raises the alarm about perceived wrongdoing within their organization to another member of their organization, this is termed 'internal' whistleblowing. External whistleblowing involves going outside of the organization to disclose—for example to a regulator or a journalist.[60] Although the two areas have traditionally been treated as somewhat separate, there is now a general consensus that whistleblowing covers both internal and external whistleblowing.[61] Nearly all external whistleblowing is preceded by whistleblowers internally raising concern about wrongdoing. Internal and external whistleblowing thus belong to the same process and should not be kept apart conceptually or from a research perspective.[62] Employees tend to blow the whistle to an external recipient when raising their concern internally is ineffective in stopping the wrongdoing or when they experience retaliation after voicing their concern. The implication is that whistleblowing to, for example, a regulator would happen only when an organization is unwilling or unable to correct its own wrongdoing. This principle is increasingly finding its way into legislation across the world.[63] A focus on the intersection of internal and external measures is key. It is generally accepted that wrongdoing in organizations should be stopped or corrected as early as possible, as this is in the interest of both organization and society. This obviously requires organizational whistleblowing arrangements that succeed in encouraging workers to speak up through channels that allow organizational actors to respond to those concerns.

Speaking Up as Voice: Prosocial or Justice-Oriented Motives? There has been a history of studying 'employee voice', defined as speaking up more frequently about problems, and improvement-oriented suggestions to superiors with the perceived power to take action[64] within organization studies particularly in the human resource management (HRM) and employee relations (ER) literatures, and within organizational behaviour (OB), although the perspectives adopted by each differ.[65] Overall, they tend to diverge on the question of what the articulation of voice represents, that is, whether it represents a challenge to problematic forms of power within the structure and management of the organization, or whether it represents an attempt to help out one's organization with the aim of improving it through addressing difficulties.[66]

Only recently have there been attempts to synthesize these different strands of literature in an integrated view and model of voice,[67] and it appears that this is a valuable exercise in the study of whistleblowing. Mowbray et al.'s[68] integrative review downplays the juxtaposition between prosocial and justice-oriented voice, for example. In their view, the distinction rests on a possibly overstated difference in motive. They argue that determining what is and what is not prosocial voice remains subjective, and that personal dissatisfaction—regarded as the trigger for justice-oriented voice—'may motivate the employee to engage in pro-social voice'.[69] Overall therefore, perhaps motivation for speaking up is less important than the fact that it happens or the recognition of the wrongdoing that prompted it. This observation is reflected in recent changes in UK law on whistleblower protection. It moved from a position where the motivation of the whistleblower was scrutinized to see whether they acted in 'good faith' or not, with protection only being promised in cases that they were. Instead in 2013 the law embraced a principle of public interest: so long as the disclosure can be shown to be in the public interest, the motivation of the whistleblower is irrelevant (see Box 2.6).

BOX 2.6   CHANGES IN PIDA

In 2013 the Public Interest Disclosure Act (PIDA) in the UK was changed to remove the condition for disclosures to be made in 'good faith'. Advocates of the change lobbied government extensively, claiming that the good faith requirement meant that organizations that were not able to prove that a disclosure had not been made were incentivized to engage in character assassination of the whistleblower. Under the amended legislation, disclosures must be made in the public interest, which has various thresholds in line with the stepped disclosure process that PIDA allows (there are more conditions that need to be met to make a disclosure externally under PIDA, and the public interest conditions parallel this, having a higher threshold for *external disclosures than internal ones). In summary, whistleblowing systems should draw the focus away from motivation, putting the spotlight on the exposing and stopping of wrongdoing instead. Speak-up arrangements that are implemented can take this into account and make motive irrelevant to how management responds.**

*For more information, see S. Musgrave and A. Dunn, (2013), Whistleblowing – Goodbye 'in good faith', Hello 'in the public interest' – and wider issues, in Bird & Bird, 21 June, available at https://www.twobirds.com/en/news/articles/2013/uk/whistleblowing-goodbye-in-good-faith-hello-in-the-public-interest--and-wider-issues.

Another Common Problem: A Lack of Attention to the Recipient's Response

Another common misunderstanding sees whistleblowing as an act, or a process, that centres around the whistleblower as an individual. In fact, whistleblowing is never an individual phenomenon; for every disclosure of wrongdoing there is a person for whom it is intended, whether they hear it or not. We know that 'responsiveness', or the assumed willingness of the assumed target of the information to listen and respond, is an important influence in whether someone will speak out in the first place, and whether the outcome is successful.[70] Management response thus has an effect on the likelihood and form of employee voice, as 'even the most proactive or satisfied employees are likely to "read the wind" as to whether it is safe and/or worthwhile to speak up'.[71] Milliken et al. found that what stops employees from voicing ideas or concerns is to some extent fear of retaliation, but that this fear was largely relational, that is, they feared they would become untrustworthy for others (bosses and peers).[72] The perceived futility of voice was also a key influence. Harlos finds that people must believe their viewpoints are being considered for voice to occur.[73] Even so however, responsiveness remains under-researched in both the voice and whistleblowing literatures.[74] Research carried out in Australia offers important insights into whistleblowers' experiences of manager responsiveness, showing how whistleblowers are likely to be satisfied with how their disclosure was handed, only if they are kept informed about the process, and they themselves are vindicated in relation to the wrongdoing.[75] This research details the difficulties in managing effective responsiveness to whistleblowing disclosures; the expectations of whistleblowers can differ vastly from those of their managers, and the people responsible for dealing with their case, for example. Researchers conclude that the initial stages of disclosure are key. Unless these are well managed and the whistleblower feels comfortable that she has been responded to appropriately, a cycle of mistrust and uncertainty can ensue. It is difficult to break this cycle. In Chapter 4, barriers to and facilitators of responsiveness that emerged from the research for this book are reflected on and discussed.

One area in which responsiveness has come to the fore involves the recent growth in studies that explore the nature of the whistleblower as a political figure, that is, one who speaks truth to power from a relative position of powerlessness. Many authors have drawn on Michel Foucault's concept of fearless speech (parrhesia), inspired by his work on Ancient Greece, in order to develop a new conception of the whistleblower as truthteller.[76] Fearless speech (see Box 2.7) has a number of features: it represents an interruption of the status quo by an act of speech of a person of lower status than those holding power.[77] Fearless statements therefore have the potential to create change by speaking out even in the context of asymmetrical power relations.[78] Fearless speech must involve an element of risk; the subject engages in truthtelling where he has 'a specific relation to truth through frankness [and] a certain type of relationship to his own life through danger ... ,'[79] and speaks up despite these known perils.[80] Translating these to the context of whistleblowing, the protagonist must be fully aware of this risk and the fact that his truthtelling might jeopardize his well-being and safety.[81] In addition to embracing risk, fearless speech involves speaking what one feels to be their 'naked' truth.[82] Finally, the fearless speaker has 'a specific relation to moral law through freedom and duty'.[83] A moral obligation spurs the fearless speakers to action.[84] As Jack notes, drawing on Foucault, 'as a mode of subjectivation, truth-telling enables the individual to establish a relation to a particular set of social norms and rules and to recognize himself as obligated to put them into practice'.[85]

BOX 2.7   EXCERPT FROM VANDEKERCKHOVE AND LANGENBERG (2012, P. 37) OVERVIEW OF PARRHESIA

Parrhesia means 'frankly speaking the truth', and stems from a moral motivation of the speaker. In this specific act, the meaning of ethics is reduced to *critique as an attitude*. In this sense, parrhesia is the localized manifestation of critique as an attitude. We can summarize Foucault's analysis of the political meaning of parrhesia developed in his lectures 1981–1984 as follows (Foucault 2001, 2009):

- Parrhesia is a necessary condition for democracy: 'Frankly speaking truth' is a necessity and is elicited by the dynamic of the agora;
- Parrhesia is done by someone who is inferior to those for whom the critical and moral motivated truth is intended;
- Parrhesia is a democratic right: as a citizen of Athens, citizens had the right and some even had a moral obligation to use parrhesia;
- Parrhesia is a necessary condition for care because caring for the self as a matter of telling yourself the truth is presupposed to be able to take care of others, of the polis;

- Parrhesia implies both having and displaying courage, because speaking truth in public presupposes the courage to contradict the prevailing discourse, the public, the sovereign. This could mean that the parrhesiastes might risk his/her life;
- Parrhesia presupposes self-critique as a precondition for a moral attitude.*

*From W. Vandekerckhove and S. Langenberg (2012), 'Can we organize courage?: Implications of Foucault's parrhesia', *Electronic Journal of Business Ethics and Organizational Studies* 17(2): pp. 35–44, referencing M. Foucault, (2001), *Cours au Collège de France. 1981–1982. L'herméneutique du sujet.* Paris, Gallimard Seuil; and M. Foucault (2009), *Cours au Collège de France. 1984. Le courage de la vérité. Le gouvernement de soi et des autres II.* Paris, Gallimard Seuil.

In short, therefore, fearless speech is appealing because it represents an 'ethico-political practice that opens up possibilities of new ways of relating to the self and others (the ethical dimension) and new ways of organizing relations to others (the political dimension)'.[86] This has important implications for speak-up systems. A notable aspect of fearless speech within organizational settings is the presence of an 'other' who is able to listen to the disruptive statement; without this, fearless speech's political impact is lost. Thus, scholars discuss the importance of the 'parrhesiastic chain' of relationality between speaker and hearer for effective truthtelling.[87] Organizations that institutionalize whistleblowing through, for example, the introduction of speak-up systems and whistleblowing hotlines run the risk of deadening fearless critique, because they systemize a process that needs to contain an element of spontaneity and surprise in order to be truly interruptive. Overly systemized approaches render the designated listener unable to hear the unexpected.[88] Kenny and her colleagues recently explored the role of parrhesia in organizational whistleblowing in some depth, as detailed in Box 2.8.

BOX 2.8   PARRHESIA AND PASSIONATE ATTACHMENTS

When thinking about fearless speech (parrhesia) it is important to note that whistleblowers often don't make a conscious, rational choice to speak the truth by calculating the risk to themselves. Rather, they make a series of ethical decisions and become whistleblowers in the process. The authors explore this, drawing inspiration from Judith Butler's work.[89] Butler articulates that although we are not autonomous but, rather, always becoming in relation to

(Continued)

powerful discourses, we still have psychic processes of desire that lead to identifications with given social norms which are both suffused with affect and allow us to be recognized as a legitimate subject.[90] That is, because we require recognition to exist socially, and because this recognition requires some stable position that is impossible (as we are always 'becoming' and influenced by powerful discourses), we latch on to norms and values so as to construct an illusory sense of a stable identity that can then be recognized.

Using this view, the authors question how whistleblower subjectivity is formed and re-formed through the attachments that shape the process of truthtelling. They find that whistleblowing in organizations is not merely bound up in its specific discursive and circumstantial context (the organizational setting and the power that is in play) but that it is an affective and socially situated emergence that emerges from the employee's passionate attachment to organizational ideals and professional norms.

In their empirical work, the authors find that the whistleblower subjects did not make a calculated choice to speak truth to power, but rather they invoked various identities and described passionate attachments to the norms that governed such subject positions. They described themselves as moving between positions such as professional, loyal organization member, outsider, and involuntary discloser while their account of these positions emerged during the interview they conducted with the researchers. They saw themselves as 'just doing their job' rather than engaging in some heroic deed. This highlights that they did not make a calculated, fully conscious decision to risk everything. Whistleblowing is not a one-off event, but rather a process that plays out over long periods of time. The authors found that the whistleblowers they interviewed trusted the organization, and the belief that their disclosures would be taken seriously played an important role in their decision to speak up. Additionally, whereas previous research had positioned whistleblowers as reinventing themselves, freed from previous organizational identities and emerging with a new, separate identity of 'whistleblower', the authors found that the ties that whistleblowers had with their previous organization were not easily shaken.[91]

These findings shed light on an important learning about fearless speech. Instead of representing an act of total freedom that is acted out by a heroic, freed subject, it is a complex practice that is acted out by emerging subjects that are organizationally attached. By emphasizing this point, the authors show that critique of power doesn't require someone that is somehow free of attachments or more willing to risk it all.

Management response, although under researched, is an important part of speaking up. Although barriers to management responsiveness are discussed in more detail in Chapter 4, if we look at whistleblowing as a form of fearless speech (parrhesia), two important lessons emerge. First is that speak-up systems that try to be too systematic will defeat the purpose, because the fearless speaker requires an element of risk, and will speak up in a spontaneous way. This means for speak-up systems to work they need to be flexible and multiple, so that those who speak are not limited by what they can disclose, and how they disclose it. The second lesson is that the response from management is a necessary part of the process. Without it, the whistleblower/fearless speaker will not speak up. They need to trust that they will be heard and responded to. This trust is another vital part of the process of speaking up, and is discussed next.

Speaking Up and Trust

Even where speak-up systems are in place, research shows us that if trust is not present, they are not likely to be used. Higher levels of trust are associated with higher usage of internal channels and higher perceptions of efficacy of these by the potential whistleblowers.[92] In fact, where trust is low, whistleblowers are more likely to go outside of their organization to disclose wrongdoing,[93] although research to date is limited. We know that success in making one's disclosure heard, and the safety of the whistleblower when doing so, are both tightly related to levels of trust.[94]

Trust is clearly a very important concept in speak-up arrangements but how should we understand it? Trust is a complex social phenomenon whose meaning varies widely depending on the person, the relationship being considered, the context surrounding it[95] and even the disciplinary tradition in which it is being examined.[96] A useful interpretation sees trust as a state of favourable expectation regarding other people's actions and intentions[97] and this is explored further in Chapter 4. As an example relevant to this book, whistleblowing happens when the person disclosing the wrongdoing cannot stop it herself and so the whistleblower (trustor) expects the recipient (trustee) to do so.

Behavioural trust—trust in people and organizations—entails aspects of both competence trust and intentional trust.[98] A whistleblower trusts the recipient is competent to stop the wrongdoing—that is, the recipient has the required technical, cognitive, and communicative competencies. In addition, a whistleblower trusts the recipient will forego opportunism and instead act honestly, truthfully, and shield the whistleblower from potential harm. Hence the whistleblower has trust in the recipient's dedication and benevolence towards them.[99] An example of the complexity of this in practice is offered in Chapter 4. There is a growing body of evidence from whistleblowing research suggesting that for employees, the belief or confidence that someone will be interested in listening and able to take action regarding the wrongdoing, is an important predictor influencing the likelihood of them speaking up.[100] Lewis[101] and Uys[102] examined employment regulations to explore how notions of trust and loyalty are interwoven in whistleblowing events, and speculated how different alternative conceptions of loyalty implicate different notions of trust.

Despite its clear relevance, trust has not generally formed a major aspect of whistleblowing research. The focus instead tends to remain on the whistleblower and the wrongdoing about which whistleblowing occurs.[103] It largely ignores the nature of the expectation the whistleblower has of the recipient of the disclosure, or how that expectation is formed. Chapter 4 discusses the expectations that speak-up entail, drawing on Watzlawick's theories. It appears, however, that we can learn much from theories of trust outside this field of inquiry.

Trust has a presence within the field of organizational culture but even here, is somewhat poorly understood. It tends to be treated as a static characteristic of organizational culture.[104] In contrast, it appears important to heed the literature from within the wider field of organization studies that sees trust as a process in which time is a key dimension for examining how trust happens and evolves through interactions between truster and trustee.[105] An example of how time influences trust is given in Chapter 4, drawing on the case studies from Chapter 3 as illustrative examples.

Trust scholars insist on the strong contingent and nontransitive properties of trust,[106] offering a model of reflexive engagement combining both rationality and emotions.[107] If we research ongoing interactions in the whistleblowing process for example, it is unreasonable to ignore that perceptions about past interactions, propensities towards opportunism, and possibilities of building trust are formed during these repeated interactions. Earlier experiences can provide small cues that, through a process of sense-making, are subsequently enlarged through accumulation of evidence, which may lead to behavioural changes instantiating alternative or additional forms of trust.[108]

For these reasons, examining how trusting in organizations changes and evolves is essential when studying trust as a process. Just as whistleblowing needs to be seen as a process (noted earlier), therefore, so also must trust be seen as something that develops over time, and that inheres to a variety of different relationships, between multiple parties that can form the 'chain of whistleblowing.' Elsewhere we show that the whistleblowing process is constituted by different trust relationships, and moreover, that speak-up operators seek to establish and maintain trusting within the whistleblowing process.[109]

The distinction between internal and external whistleblowing was introduced, and problematized earlier. An important implication for studying trust in the context of whistleblowing is that differentiation between different recipients of the disclosure needs to be made. Someone might not trust the compliance officer in the organization to act upon the whistleblowing, for example, but might have trust in one of the board members to do so. Research into whistleblowing recipients has predominantly used an internal/external dichotomy with little or no differentiation within these categories[110] although Kaptein's study, which is discussed in depth in Chapter 4, is an exception.

It appears clear that research into organizational interventions aimed at supporting trust between whistleblowers and internal recipients is vital. The implementation of speak-up arrangements in organizations represents a management intervention. These are often linked to stated values and rules of the organization in codes of conduct.[111] Möllering's sketch of the process view 'trusting as constituting' suggests, however, that trusting is not simply dependent on the organizational context—that is, the trusting that emerges around speak-up arrangements is not determined by the conjoining values statement.[112] Trusting as constituting also implies that rules and resources in which speak-up arrangements are embedded (such as organizational values) are (re)produced.

Research into Speak-up Arrangements

Speak-up arrangements as organizational policies and procedures for internal whistleblowing have rarely been researched[113] and when they are, little to no differentiation is made between the various designs and embedment of such arrangements.[114] This might be because they are a relatively new phenomenon.

Although relatively scarce, it is interesting to examine the small body of research into how speak-up processes are being implemented in organizations. We know that figures are still low: with the general figure for UK companies being 23%, just over 30% in Ireland,[115] and 28% in the United States. In the Australian public sector, speak-up systems have been a requirement for a number of years but even so, their implementation and use has been patchy, lacking guidance for employees, and training for managers for example.[116] In relation to hotlines, we know that the use of this method to facilitate workers raising a concern is increasing: in 2010 less than half of organizations worldwide had a hotline in place[117] and in 2018 that had risen to an average per region of 63%.[118]

Gaps persist however: no clear data exist on how many of these hotlines are operated by an external provider, and little is known about precise characteristics of such arrangements or what the current trend might be. An exception to this is the groundbreaking research being carried out into public and private sector whistleblowing in Australia.[119] What we do know is that in the public sector, externally operated hotlines are rarely used. In the UK's NHS Trusts for example, whistleblowing procedures mention an externally provided helpline for speaking up about wrongdoing (operated by MenCap), but the policies do not prescribe this route to actually raise a concern.[120] Vandekerckhove and Lewis[121] find that official guidelines for organizational whistleblowing arrangements are not consistent about whether hotlines or other organizational whistleblowing arrangements should even be operated by an external provider in the first place. On the other hand, Vandekerckhove and Rumyantseva[122] found that NHS managers started to rethink their organizational whistleblowing arrangements in response to workers bringing their concern immediately to the regulator before raising it inside the organization. Research into internal auditors acting as whistleblowers in public services in Indonesia found a much higher likelihood and willingness for them to report wrongdoing using internal channels.[123]

In relation to the internal/external distinction commonly used to describe whistleblowing procedures, it appears that the situation is slightly more complex—the divide can be somewhat unclear. Research in the UK on 1,000 cases of whistleblowers calling the Public Concern at Work advice line[124] shows that workers tend to raise their concern first with their line manager (52%), versus 22% with higher management, and 7% to an external agency. Only 4% raised their concern initially with internal audit or via a hotline. Of those that raised their concern a second time, 33% did so with higher management, 23% with an external agency (of which 11% regulator, and 11% with a professional body), whereas 10% raised it with internal audit or through a hotline. At a third attempt, 21% raised their concern with a regulator, 14% with audit or through a hotline, and 14% with a professional body (see also Chapter 4). We note that the use of internal audit and hotlines increases in a similar pattern as that of regulators and professional bodies. This suggests that, as the whistleblowing process unfolds, the whistleblower tends to seek a recipient that shows independence, rather than merely shifting from internal to external whistleblowing. To further complicate the internal/external divide, whereas compliance officers in private sector organizations perceive using an externally operated hotline as external whistleblowing, this would still be regarded as internal whistleblowing from the regulator's and the UK PIDA point of view. Hence internal and external speak-up arrangements require both attention and research to ensure that they are effective.

Finally, speak-up arrangements are often used in unintended and unpredictable ways. They are typically instituted by management in an attempt to make employee voice a part of its human resource management agenda.[125] However, this does not always play out in practice; recent research shows that speak-up arrangements designed by management are not merely used by employees in the way and for purposes intended by management.[126] Voice channels explicitly designated for compliance-related concerns are also used by employees to voice grievances, for example.

The issue of an internal champion has been central in debates on what comprises an effective speak-up system and yet has been woefully overlooked. Referring to scholars interested in speak-up systems, de Graaf notes that 'we know least about those factors we can most easily influence', referring to the role of the confidential integrity advisor (CIA).[127] (See Box 2.9.)

BOX 2.9   THE SPEAK-UP CHAMPION

De Graaf et al. study the most effective internal reporting systems and focus in particular on the role that the confidential integrity advisor should play. They draw on a variety of data sources including interviews with 25 CIAs from across a range of public organizations, and a survey with Dutch civil servants (n = 7543). Their findings show that CIAs are an important part of internal whistleblowing procedures. Specifically, the more emphasis and value is placed on the CIAs, the more reports are made to them, whereas the organizations that only have them because they are required by law, and therefore invest minimal effort in training and promoting them as a resource for staff receive very few reports through this channel.

There is some ambiguity around the CIA role, as legislation has left it open on purpose to allow them to fit the needs of a wide range of organizations, but this approach has its downfalls. Although having an undefined role has led many CIAs to become more of a sounding board, offering advice to those that are reporting, this often leaves the CIA in a difficult place, because they are accountable to the organization even though most feel that their loyalty should lie with the reporters. Issues with confidentiality also come up, because CIA's are required to report some integrity issues to law enforcement, and subsequent lawsuits always identify the reporter to the wrongdoer.

Overall, De Graaf finds that the CIA, when properly trained and supported by management, is a valuable resource for those who wish to report wrongdoing. Where this function is combined with the Confidential Harassment Adviser (CHA) they are able to be catch all points of contact for people to come to when they have encountered various types of wrongdoing. Champions who are now required in financial services in various country contexts can learn from the example of CIAs in the Netherlands. http://www.tandfonline.com/doi/full/10.1080/10967494.2015.1094163

De Graaf finds that CIAs can play an essential role in ensuring that the reporting system is effective, albeit that they must enjoy management support if this is to be the case. CIAs must also have unambiguous descriptions of their tasks and responsibilities along with support from their own line managers.

In addition, empirical research into factors precipitating whistleblowing by compliance officers in the financial services sector,[128] indicates that the issue of power (to control, to intervene, to protect—managers as well as workers), and the culture of the organization in place also appear to be vital drivers in the success of a speak-up arrangement. In their joint research on whistleblowing in banking, defense contracting services as well as health and social care, the authors found that the structure and set-up of an organization may facilitate or impede internal and/or external reporting of wrongdoing.[129] Furthermore, the individual's role within it can also impact on their sense of responsibility in disclosing information about illegal activities.[130] In these studies it appears that overall, most whistleblowers attempted initially to report wrongdoing through internal structures although some proceeded through such reporting structures up to a point where it became clear to them that no actions would be taken to correct the wrongdoing.

Effective Speak-up Arrangements: Towards a New Framework

As shown earlier, research into speak-up arrangements is rare, but what research there is shows that speak-up arrangements are not common in organizations, with less than one-third reporting that formal channels are in place in any given study. The research that does exist shows that there is not a clear divide on internal and external disclosures and highlights that both internal and external speak-up arrangements require attention and research to ensure that they are effective. The implementation of hotlines is increasing, but whistleblowers still disclose internally multiple times before resorting to external options. Finally, speak-up arrangements are often used in unintended and unpredictable ways, and employees use these channels to speak up about a range of topics, some of which fall outside whistleblowing issues.

What we discuss next will hopefully help guide those in charge of implementing speak-up arrangements toward policies that are informed and effective. Successful organizational whistleblowing arrangements are those that overcome barriers for workers to raise a concern with other organizational actors, as well as remove obstacles for organizational actors who receive whistleblower concerns to initiate action and correct wrongdoing. Our conceptual approach considers whistleblowing as a social construct that depends on the interaction of people within an organization and its social setting.[131] In relation to what constitutes effective speak-up arrangements, existing research highlights the importance of perceived responsiveness to the whistleblower's contact,[132] perceived trust in both the independence of the recipient of the information,[133] and in the communication integrity.

Analysis of the aforementioned literature leads us to regard the crucial variables in determining the benefits, challenges and best practices associated with internal and/or external types of whistleblowing arrangement to be culture, responsiveness, trust and power. These were incorporated within our research aims and the design of the case studies as described in Chapter 3.

These background issues give rise to important areas of concern in studying effective speak-up policies and systems, including:

- What factors enable effective whistleblowing as part of a speak-up process, from an organizational, design and implementation perspective?
- Can we better understand the distinction between internal and external procedures, which is in practice somewhat blurred and requiring definition and explication? How can we design systems accordingly?
- What are the key challenges to effective speak-up policies, including the major organizational, structural and cultural obstacles to speaking up through speak-up arrangements?
- What are the best practices associated with effective speak-up arrangements, drawing on cross-sector learning?

ENDNOTES

1. Hersh (2002); Grant (2021).
2. Near and Miceli (1985: 4);
3. For a useful overview see Lewis and Vandekerckhove (2015).
4. Kaptein (2011); Loyens and Maesschalck (2014); Vandekerckhove, Brown, and Tsahuridu (2014); Weber and Wasielski (2013).
5. Heffernan (2012); Milliken et al. (2003).
6. See Public Concern at Work (2014); Vandekerckhove and Lewis (2012).
7. Council of Europe (2014); Devine (2015); EU Commission (2018).
8. For a useful overview see Lewis and Vandekerckhove (2015); cf. Coleman (2015) for such a call from the Securities and Exchange Commission in the United States, and FCA (2015b) for the Financial Conduct Authority in the UK.
9. FCA (2015b).
10. Francis (2015); Lewis and Vandekerckhove (2015).
11. PCAW (2013). Since 2018, PCAW has been renamed Protect.
12. BIS (2015).
13. Bjørkelo (2013); Mesmer-Magnus and Viswesvaran (2005); Rehg et al. (2008).
14. Miceli and Near (1992); Ethics Resource Centre (2014).
15. Rehg et al. (2008: 222).
16. Martin and Rifkin (2004); Miethe (1999).
17. Bolsin et al. (2005); Near et al. (1993).
18. General Medical Council (2015).
19. Burrows (2001); Premeaux and Bedeian (2003); Smith and Brown (2008).
20. Ewing (1983).
21. Armenakis (2004: 359).
22. Ibid.
23. Alford (2007).

24. Kenny (2019).
25. Ibid.
26. See Lennane (1996/2012); Miethe (1999); Parmerlee et al. (1982) for a comprehensive overview.
27. Ethics Resource Centre (2012); Lennane (1996/2012); Mesmer-Magnus and Viswesvaran (2005); Rothschild and Miethe (1999); Vandekerckhove, Brown, and Tsahuridu (2014).
28. Martin and Rifkin (2004).
29. Worth (2013).
30. Jubb (1999); Near and Miceli (1985).
31. Thomas (2005: 147).
32. For example, Grant (2002).
33. Hersh (2002).
34. Mesmer-Magnus and Viswesvaran (2005); Near, Dworkin, and Miceli (1993).
35. Mesmer-Magnus and Viswesvaran (2005); Rothschild (2013).
36. van der Velden et al. (2018).
37. Rothschild and Miethe (1999).
38. Rothschild (2013: 653).
39. Alford (2001:104).
40. Bjørkelo (2013).
41. Jackson et al. (2010); Peters et al. (2011).
42. Lennane (1993).
43. Rothschild (2013: 653).
44. Lennane (1996/2012: 257).
45. Lennane (1996/2012).
46. Alford (2001); Rothschild and Miethe (1999).
47. Corrigan (2005).
48. Kenny, Fotaki, and Scriver (2018).
49. Fotaki, Kenny, and Scriver (2015).
50. Martin and Rifkin (2004).
51. Bowers et al. (2012).
52. Vandekerckhove (2006).
53. Ibid.
54. Kaptein (2011).
55. Alford (2001); Glazer and Glazer (1991).
56. Vandekerckhove and Phillips (2017).
57. Vandekerckhove and Phillips (2017).
58. Ibid.
59. Kenny (2018).
60. See, e.g., Jubb (1999); Detert and Burris (2007); Pohler and Luchak (2014).
61. Lewis, Brown, and Moberly (2014).
62. Miceli, Near, and Dworkin (2008); Vandekerckhove (2006); Vandekerckhove and Phillips (2017).
63. Vandekerckhove (2010); Council of Europe (2014).
64. Burris et al. (2017); Detert and Burris (2007); Dutton et al. (1997).
65. Burris (2012); Liang et al. (2012); Maynes and Podsakoff (2014); Morrison (2011).

66. Barry and Wilkinson (2016); Mesmer-Magnus and Viswesvaran (2005); Morrison (2011); Miceli, Near, and Dworkin (2008); Sims and Keenan (1998).
67. Klaas et al. (2012); Mowbray et al. (2015).
68. Mowbray et al. (2015).
69. Mowbray et al (2015: 388).
70. Burris (2012); Rothschild and Miethe (1999).
71. Detert and Burris (2007: 869).
72. Milliken et al. (2003).
73. Harlos (2001).
74. Vandekerckhove et al. (2014). Where it has received attention, the way in which management responds to employee voice has mainly been studied as an 'independent variable', that is, the focus is on how it *affects other actions*, rather than it being the topic of study in its own right.
75. Smith and Brown (2008).
76. Andrade (2015); Jones et al. (2005); Mansbach (2009); Rothschild (2013).
77. Contu (2014); Mansbach (2009); Weiskopf and Tobias-Miersch (2016: 650).
78. Mansbach (2009).
79. Foucault (2001: 19).
80. Foucault (2010); see Weiskopf and Wilmott (2013: 483).
81. See Andrade (2015); Jack (2004); Weiskopf and Tobias-Miersch (2016); Mansbach (2011) for a discussion of this in organization studies literature.
82. Foucault (2005: 382); see also Mansbach (2009); Jones et al. (2005); Rothschild (2013) for a discussion of this in organizational whistleblowing.
83. Foucault (2001: 19).
84. Weiskopf and Tobias-Miersch (2016: 652).
85. Jack (2004: 130).
86. Weiskopf and Tobias-Miersch (2016: 650).
87. Vandekerckhove and Langenberg (2012); Weiskopf and Tobias-Miersch (2016: 657); Vandekerckhove et al. (2014); Kenny et al. (2019).
88. Vandekerckhove and Langenberg (2012); see also Contu (2014).
89. Kenny et al. (2019).
90. Butler (1997).
91. Alford (2007); Weiskopf and Tobias-Mierch (2016).
92. Near and Miceli (1985).
93. Binikos (2006).
94. Holtzhausen (2009).
95. Lane and Bachmann (1998).
96. Fotaki (2014).
97. Möllering (2001: 404).
98. Nooteboom (1996; 2006).
99. See, for example, Brown and Donkin (2008).
100. Cassematis and Wortley (2013); Transparency International Ireland (2017); Vandekerckhove et al. (2014).
101. Lewis (2011).
102. Uys (2008).
103. Vandekerckhove et al. (2014).
104. Holtzhausen (2009); Lewis (2011); Near and Miceli (1985); Uys (2008).

105. Bachman et al. (2015); Laan et al. (2011); Möllering (2001, 2006, 2013); Nooteboom (1996, 2006); Saunders et al. (2014).
106. Barbalet (2009).
107. Möllering (2006).
108. Adobor (2005); Jagd (2010).
109. Vandekerckhove, Fotaki, Kenny, Humantito, and Ozdemir Kaya (2016).
110. Vandekerckhove and Phillips (2017).
111. Moberly and Wiley (2011); Vandekerckhove and Commers (2004).
112. Möllering (2013).
113. Burris (2012).
114. Harlos (2001); Mowbray et al. (2015).
115. Transparency International Ireland (2017).
116. Brown et al. (2016).
117. Central and South America leading with 52.9%, Oceania closing with 26.0%; Asia-Pacific leading at 62.7%, Middle East and North Africa last with 44.9%.
118. ACFE (2010, 2018).
119. Smith and Brown (2008); Roberts et al. (2011).
120. Vandekerckhove and Rumyantseva (2014).
121. Vandekerckhove and Lewis (2012).
122. Vandekerckhove and Rumyantseva (2014).
123. Fotaki and Humantito (2015).
124. Vandekerckhove, James, and West (2013).
125. Barry and Wilkinson (2016); Vandekerckhove and Langenberg (2012).
126. Vandekerckhove, Kenny, Fotaki, Humantito, and Ozdemir Kaya (2016).
127. de Graaf (2016: 2).
128. Kenny (2014).
129. Vandekerckhove, Kenny, Fotaki, Humantito, and Ozdemir Kaya (2016).
130. Ibid; Fotaki, and Humantito (2015).
131. Vandekerckhove (2010).
132. Kenny (2014).
133. Rothschild and Miethe (1999); Keenan (1995).

CHAPTER 3

A Comparative Study of Speak-up Arrangements in Banking, Engineering, and Healthcare Sectors

INTRODUCTION

As mentioned in Chapter 2, the most common definition of whistleblowing is 'the disclosure by organization members (former or current) of illegal, immoral, or illegitimate practices under the control of their employers, to persons or organizations that may be able to effect action'.[1,2] The concerns whistleblowers raise range from ethically questionable behaviour to clearly illegal activity with a (significant) grey area between the two.[3] As this chapter will demonstrate through examples, such behaviour usually results from or is built into organizational and social structures; it can be a part of the 'normal' way of life. Therefore, some whistleblowers inevitably 'go(es) against group norms and attempt(s) to change improper group behaviour'.[4] Even though a whistleblower acts in the greater interests of the collective, challenging a normative order—established group norms—is often met with negative reactions.[5] An infamous example is the NHS in the UK that 'can in effect act as a monopoly when it comes to excluding staff from employment'.[6] Whistleblowers can suffer many personal costs including bullying at work, social exclusion, loss of employment, enduring lengthy and expensive legal battles, and detriment to mental health.

Evidence suggests that effective speak-up arrangements can provide support systems for whistleblowers while gathering information that can be used to further organizational and public interest. Without these mechanisms, valuable whistleblowing information is not effectively received and acted upon. As noted earlier in this book, whistleblowing has exposed fraud that has cost companies a

significant amount of money. Yet, speak-up arrangements offer even more significant benefits than financial savings, such as prevention of environmental disasters,
serious workplace accidents, and threats to patient safety in health care settings.
This realisation led to a 10% increase in implementation of speak-up arrangements
in public and private organizations between 2012 and 2015,[7] with the Financial
Conduct Authority (FCA) in the UK reporting a '72% increase in the number
of investigations into the conduct of regulated financial companies opened as a
result of a tipoff from a whistleblower'.[8] Although overall implementation rates
are still low (see Chapter 2), it is encouraging to see that there is momentum in
this area.

While a growing number of organizations implement speak-up arrangements
and speak-up reports are on the increase, the satisfaction of voicing employees
with the outcome of raising a concern has been decreasing since 2012, with less
than two-fifths claiming to be satisfied.[9] In this context, it is more important than
ever to identify best practice in speak-up design and operation. With this in mind,
we conducted a comparative study of three organizations with considerable experience in speak-up arrangements: a healthcare organization (an NHS Trust in the
UK), a multinational bank, and a multinational engineering firm.

In this chapter we analyse common types of wrongdoing, the state of speak-up
systems in each sector, and how internal speak-up arrangements for each industry
case relate to the political and economic context. We then draw lessons and outline
best practices based on evidence.[10] First, we analyse the banking sector in which
'creative accounting',[11] rule-gaming[12] and tax avoidance are the most pressing
issues. Here, we give a brief account of neoliberalism and financial capitalism
that provides the economic and political backdrop to all the cases we researched.
The second case is from the engineering sector, where corruption can enter the
picture when big projects are commissioned by public authorities. Also, health
and safety is a prominent concern in this sector, so regulators play a more active
role. Lastly, we analyse a public healthcare organization, where tackling threats
to patient safety is at the top of speak-up operators' agenda. Here, highly regulated and complex organizational structures, operating under financial pressure
and close public scrutiny, present unique challenges.

BANKING

In the past four decades, the financial sector has grown rapidly as can be seen in
its increased contribution to GDP (see Figure 3.1), the total size of physical and
financial assets owned by financial firms, and the growing number of employees.[13]
In the course of three decades preceding the 2008 financial crisis, the sector had
been restructured through globalisation, technological innovation, and deregulation that led to invention of complex and high-risk financial instruments such as
subprime mortgages, securities and derivatives.[14] Due to their lucrative nature,

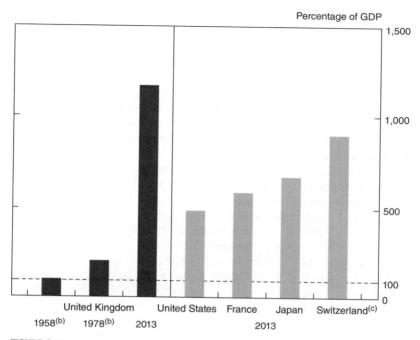

Percentage of GDP

FIGURE 3.1 Chart showing the increase in GDP represented by financial sector activity. Source: Adapted from Burrows, Low, and Cumming (2015).

banks entered into fierce competition to trade in these products, on which their competitiveness gradually became dependent. In the US, for example, trading in derivatives grew from $106 trillion in 2001, to $531 trillion in 2008.[15]

Increased use of new and highly complex financial instruments challenged the legal and technological infrastructure as well as making risk analysis almost impossible for both banks and the regulators.[16] The focus of organizational policies and culture in banks had also shifted from risk management to aggressive sales strategies.[17] This eroded the authority of the compliance function whose concerns often conflicted with the ambitions of the sales department.[18] This increased risk-taking should have raised a red flag but was overlooked by policy-makers, regulators and representatives of the industry due to a strong ideological conviction in the capacity of the sector to self regulate.[19]

The effectiveness of self-regulated markets has proven to be more of a myth than reality, as evidenced by recurring crises in capitalism since its inception. Each of these catastrophic events has led to public outcry for regulators to step in to protect the public interest and prevent similar events in the future. Public authorities try to ensure the stability of financial markets through 'prudential supervision of financial firms'[20] by, for example, enforcing a solvency ratio, that is, the ratio of their equity to their outstanding loans, that usually stands at 8% or more.[21] To do this, however, regulators depend on public accounts disclosed by financial firms to examine their solvency.[22] Because the firms prepare their own accounts, there can exist a range of deceptive practices through which organizations can misrepresent their financial performance.[23] For example, figures can be manipulated to misrepresent equity and liabilities. Most private organizations engaged with this type of 'creative accounting'[24] are mainly concerned with seeming to generate more income than they actually do in order to attract investment or increase their credit rating. For financial firms, however, the main driver is the desire to hide the volume of risk they assume. Complex financial instruments and operations, therefore, provide a fertile ground for financial engineering to circumvent regulation.

In this environment, it is particularly challenging for regulators to examine derivatives, which are 'financial instruments such as options, futures and other contracts whose value is linked to some underlying financial instrument or index'.[25] They are mostly unregulated entities and can be utilised to mask financial contingencies.[26] Mergers and acquisitions, which increased exponentially in the run-up to the 2008 crisis, also pose challenges as they require 'consolidation'[27] of accounts belonging to separate entities. Consolidation is a set of techniques employed to represent merging accounts into a single financial statement. Regulations provide general guidance as to the relative weight each account should have in the resulting statement but leave scope for case-specific judgment necessitated by the sheer complexity of each real life situation.[28] This unfortunately leaves room for 'creative accounting'[29] often in the form of manipulating the ratio of assets to liabilities.

BOX 3.1   REGULATING THE FINANCIAL SECTOR

John Snow was the 73rd US Secretary of the Treasury, serving under President George W. Bush from 2003 to 2006. He resigned under a cloud of scandal when it was uncovered that Snow failed to pay income taxes on the $24 million of loan forgiveness he received while CEO of CSX Corporation, and he was succeeded by Henry Paulsen, the CEO of Goldman Sachs, in 2006.

In 2008, he gave testimony to the Committee on Oversight and Government Reform, who were investigating role of regulators in the 2008 Financial Crisis. In his testimony he said:

Thank you, Congressman Davis. It seems to me the root issue here, when you get right down to it, is risk and leverage. Nowhere in our financial regulatory system is there anyone with full accountability and full 360-degree view on that proposition, risk and leverage. I saw that in my days at the Treasury Department. I remember in 2005 sensing that there were developments in the debt markets, the subprime and the mortgage markets that needed to be better understood. I took what was deemed to be a fairly extraordinary step and called in all of the substantive regulators of the mortgage market. I asked them to give their considered views on whether or not undue risk was being created. We didn't yet have a housing crisis. We didn't yet have a subprime crisis. But I wanted to get their view; that did eventually lead to new guidance to the regulators. But the Congressman was quoting me that no one of them had that view. They had pieces of the puzzle. It's like the blind man and the elephant. They are all touching a piece of it, but they don't know what the big picture is.

By his own admission, John Snow, the head of the US Treasury, did not have a full idea of what was going on in the financial markets leading up to the crash. Not only that, but few regulators had either. There was a lack of accountability and a complete absence of oversight in the way that debts and mortgages were being handled. In addition, just as Snow started to assemble a fuller picture, he was made to give up his role and was replaced by an industry insider.[30]

The instruments and techniques discussed earlier create a permissive environment for wrongdoing, ranging from unmistakably illegal activities, such as money laundering, to ethically questionable accounting practices that may add up to catastrophic results. The compliance function plays a vital role in preventing wrongdoing that violates legal regulations and/or professional standards. Nevertheless, its lower positioning within the organizational hierarchy and a lack of effective speak-up arrangements prevent concerns from being effectively raised and acted upon.[31] Failing to prevent wrongdoing can lead to the collapse of the entire sector. The sector as a whole is made up of a highly complex web of debtor-creditor relationships (see Box 3.1), so reputational damage to one firm can lead to a loss of trust in other financial institutions.[32] This was evidenced in 2008 when the collapse of the investment bank Lehman Brothers snowballed into a full-blown global economic crisis. The number of failed banks since 2008 in the United States alone was: 25 in 2008, 140 in 2009, 157 in 2010, 92 in 2011, 51 in 2012, 24 in 2013, 18 in 2014, 8 in 2015 and 5 in 2016.[33] Comparison of these numbers to the 10 bank failures in total that occurred between 2003 and 2007 helps put the amount of damage to the sector in perspective.[34]

Wrongdoing in the banking sector has serious consequences for societies, especially when it is as systemic as it has repetitively proven to be through recent crises and scandals.[35] The global cost of the 2008 crisis, in which financial engineering and creative accounting played a major role, is estimated at $200 trillion.[36] The public ultimately shouldered this financial burden because taxpayers' contributions were used to bail-out bankrupted banks, and economies suffered from a serious recession with long-lasting effects such as high levels of unemployment and wage freezes. At the same time, recent scandals such as HSBC Leaks and Luxleaks have unveiled the involvement of banks in tax evasion and money laundering. The latter has revealed that 340 multinational corporations channeled their profits through Luxembourg to benefit from secret deals offering lower tax rates.[37] These financial activities have stripped the countries in which these corporations operated of billions of pounds. Adding insult to injury, this is happening at a time when public services are on the brink of collapse due to years of austerity measures, which have forced the public to pick up the bill for the financial crisis.

Speak-out in the Banking Sector

In the aftermath of the financial crisis and scandals discussed in the previous section, preventing wrongdoing is now higher on the agenda for states and professional bodies.[38] Commentators have emphasised that eradicating wrongdoing in the financial sector will require joint action by employers and employees to create an organizational context that is conducive to speaking up.[39] However, the sector is known to have a culture of silence and secrecy.[40] According to the literature, the primary reasons behind the pervasiveness of silence are organizations' failure to investigate claims, retaliation against voicing employees, social isolation of voicing employees from colleagues, and gagging clauses,[41] each of which are briefly discussed next.

Previous research shows that concerns are often disregarded by line managers, who are usually the first point of contact for voicing employees, and that escalation of concerns is difficult within the strict hierarchy of banks.[42] Even if a concern is eventually investigated, investigations can lack rigour.[43] Furthermore, management typically fails to act upon reports resulting from investigations by compliance personnel and internal auditors.[44] It has also been observed that whistleblowers perversely become the object of investigation, instead of the concern they raise.[45] Their intention, personality and mental health are closely scrutinised to divert attention from the concern and discredit the whistleblower[46,47] (see the case of Eileen Foster in Chapter 2).

In their five-year review, Public Concern at Work notes that among finance professionals who called its advice line, 33% had been suspended and 31% had been dismissed for raising a concern.[48] This was higher than the averages across other sectors, which stood at 27% and 23%, respectively.[49] Another survey showed that of 500 finance professionals who participated, only 35% were confident that they would not face retaliation if they raised a concern.[50] Types of retaliation observed in financial firms range from character assassination to dismissal, causing distress to those who speak up and dissuading others who may consider speaking up.[51] (See Box 3.2.)

BOX 3.2 'SILENCE IN THE CITY': KEY FINDINGS FROM SURVEYS ON FINANCIAL SERVICES WORKERS BY PCAW AND LABATON SUCHAROW (2015)

The global financial services sector faced major changes after the financial crisis. After such a failing with extreme consequences, regulation was introduced to change the culture of the industry. In 2014/2015 surveys showed that investor confidence had returned, but insider attitudes to corruption had not changed much at all. Below are some of the prominent statistics in surveys from Labaton Sucharow and Public Concern at Work with regards to the Financial Services sector in the United States and the United Kingdom.

- *1 in 10 respondents have signed or been asked to sign a confidentiality agreement that effectively prevents them from being able to report illegal or unethical activities to the authorities. This rises to 1 in 4 for those making over $500,000 annually (Labaton Sucharow, 2015).*

- *The number of people who think their fellow employees have engaged in illegal or unethical behaviour to get ahead doubled in three years: 23% in 2015 as compared to 12% in 2012.*

- *24% of respondents in the United States, and 32% in the UK say they would likely engage in insider trading to earn $10 million if there was no chance they would get caught.*

- *32% of respondents believe that their compensation structure or bonus plan incentivizes employees to compromise ethics or break the law.*

Although there has been a decline in the number of people witnessing misconduct, there are still plenty of employees that see wrongdoing. PCAW compiled data on callers from the financial services to their advice line between 2007 and 2012 and also found the culture had not changed much:

- *Those who spoke up said nothing had been done to address their concern: 77% said this after raising their concern for the first time; this*

(Continued)

figure falls slightly to 71% after the concern is raised for a second time and is 53% when the concern was raised for a third or fourth time.

- *Though 38% of callers were either at management or executive level, 86% of wrongdoers were seen as more powerful than the whistleblower.*
- *62% of workers raised a concern at least once. This is higher than findings from other sectors (44%). However, those in financial services were less likely to raise a concern a second time (20%), which is much lower than our findings on all sectors (39%).*

This may be because whistleblowers in this sector aren't treated well:

- *In 60% of cases whistleblowers reported no response from management, either negative or positive. From the remaining 40% (112 cases).*
- *Of whistleblowers, 42% were dismissed after raising their concern for the first time. This is markedly different to previous research, where 24% of whistleblowers reported being dismissed on raising a concern for the first time.*
- *Of workers in financial services 48% reported that they were dismissed on the second attempt to raise a concern, compared to 29% from all sectors.*
- *Finally, 21% are formally disciplined, rising to 28% the second time a concern is raised.*

Source: PCAW Silence in the City (2013); Labaton Sucharow (2015).

A pervasive form of victimisation in the financial sector is social isolation. As mentioned in the beginning of this chapter, previous research has found that there is a strong ideological conviction in the ability of financial markets to self-regulate, and this over-confidence leads to underestimation of the risks posed by new financial instruments and practices.[52] Such conviction finds its expression in organizations as 'groupthink',[53] which does not allow alternative ways of thinking to be explored and contrarian views to be expressed. Challenging organizational norms, even for the purposes of compliance with legal regulations and professional standards, often results in isolation from colleagues.[54]

The last notorious barrier to speaking up in the sector involves gagging clauses. These are confidentiality agreements between employers and employees designed to prevent the latter from disclosing information about organizational practices. Although legal protections and obligations may override gagging clauses, they still deter many employees from escalating concerns to regulators as they fear the consequences that these agreements convey.[55]

These barriers to speaking up have featured in recent whistleblowing cases that garnered media attention. In 2007, Hervé Falciani, an IT consultant for HSBC bank in Geneva, Switzerland, leaked details of thousands of clients' accounts, alleging that the bank facilitated tax evasion and money laundering.[56] The documents were submitted to the French authorities, who later passed them onto other countries for whom the information was relevant.[57] Since then, several countries have conducted investigations into tax evasion and money laundering with the continued collaboration of Falciani.[58] Falciani claims that he followed his organization's speak-up arrangements and first raised his concerns internally, but the organization failed to investigate. The Swiss authorities, however, have taken him to court for stealing data with the intention of profit making, and he was sentenced to five years in prison.[59] As such, his case seems to exemplify the 'failure to investigate' discussed earlier.

Another recent well-known whistleblowing case from the financial sector is LuxLeaks. This time two (former) employees of PricewaterhouseCoopers (PwC), an auditing firm, leaked documents evidencing advance tax agreements between the Grand Duchy of Luxemburg and 340 companies, most of them multinationals.[60] These tax agreements allowed the companies to funnel profits made across the globe through Luxemburg where they would only pay about 1% in taxes, which is much lower than what they would pay in the countries where the income is generated.[61] While the LuxLeaks whistleblowers have started a global debate about tax evasion and triggered policy changes in several countries, they were 'found guilty of data theft and breach of commercial confidentiality'[62] by the court. This verdict was overturned for one of the whistleblowers, Antoine Deltour,[63] in January 2018, but not for Raphael Halet,[64] who was given a nine-month jail sentence and a €1,000 fine.

Halet had previously signed a contract with PwC which threatened him and his wife with damages of €10 million and the repossession of their home if they ever spoke about their role in the LuxLeaks scandal. The document also forbade him from questioning the validity of the court's decision in Metz to provide a bailiff access to his home and emails, despite an 1881 French law that specifically protects journalists' sources.[65] Halet claimed that he gave conflicting testimonies during the investigation fearing the consequences of this gagging clause, which might have led to his later conviction.[66]

It was the growing public pressure following these and similar successive scandals that led governments to look for ways to protect whistleblowers and make the best of the information they provide. For instance, in July 2015, the FCA has introduced new regulation for financial firms which includes the requirement to:

- Establish internal speak-up arrangements.
- Emphasise in contracts and settlement agreements that workers cannot be gagged from making a public interest disclosure.
- Inform employees about their right to raise their concerns with FCA and the Prudential Regulation Authority (PRA).[67]

PCAW has stated that the new regulation has already helped encourage speaking-up in the sector.[68] This was reflected in the number of financial sector professionals who called their advice line in 2015, which was double the amount in the previous year.[69] The callers' concerns included 'falsifying invoices and expenses, breach of data protection, incorrect reporting to a third party, misuse of client funds and market abuse'.[70] In the United States, the number of concerns raised with Office of the Whistleblower (OWB) has also increased, from 334 in the 2011 fiscal year to 3238 in the 2013 fiscal year.[71] Concerns included corporate disclosures of financials, facilitating fraud, and manipulation.[72] These indicators suggest that the culture of silence in the financial services may gradually be changed. Improvements in legal protection, regulatory oversight, and internal speak-up arrangements appear to encourage more people to expose wrongdoing.

Case in Focus

The bank we researched operates and is headquartered in Northwest Europe with some presence in the United States and eastern Europe. Its services span personal, business and corporate banking. It was established in the second half of the twentieth century and acquired and merged with other banks in the 1980s and 1990s. Together with its counterparts at the time, it was heavily engaged in commercial property lending before the 2008 crisis and was severely affected by this event.

In early 2000s, the bank's reputation suffered from successive scandals. One of these was a highly publicised case of creative accounting at one of its subsidiaries. In order to recover from the reputational loss and prevent similar events in the future, the bank developed a code of conduct. The speak-up policy formed an integral part of this code. In developing the policy, the board was particularly interested in addressing conflicts of interest, which were widespread at the time according to a speak-up operator:

> *It was at a time when there [were] very high levels of sensitivity around people, particularly at management level in the bank, being involved in —becoming involved in—conflict of interest situations with (property) developers. (...) and it had been quite clear that a lot of people involved in the bank had become involved with buying their own buy-to-lets[73] — as many of us did. (...) But some people did actually get involved in development and there were some conflict of interest situations. So there was a very, very strong message that went out from the board to say, 'We have a conflict of interest policy. You need to put your hand up now and identify if you are in any of these types of situations'.*

Initially, the speak-up channel was owned by the compliance function but had been taken over by human resources at group level after a comprehensive review undertaken after a number of years. The review was partly motivated by the board's concern to change the tone around speaking-up: from policing towards engagement. The speak-up operator continued:

> *The difference then was that the speak-up process and line and email was owned by compliance. And it was owned by compliance up until about 2012 because it travelled with our code of business ethics, now known as our code of conduct. And the ownership of the code moved in 2012 from compliance to HR. (. . .) It wasn't handled particularly well because compliance are not experts in communication. So the board said, 'Here, HR, you do it'.*

As part of the review process two charities specialising in whistleblowing and business ethics were invited to benchmark the new whistleblowing policy and help with implementing best practice. A speak-up operator said 'we are confident, again, that our current speak-up, which had some minor changes in it, addresses all the requirements of that new [regulator's acronym] policy document'. The code of conduct and the speak-up arrangement continue to be reviewed annually.

The speak-up arrangements allow employees to raise concerns with their line manager, internal 'key persons' (the CEO, chairman, HR director, head of internal audit, chief risk officer, and the head of compliance), through an internally operated hotline and email. The bank also has a contract with an external independent advice line, which provides guidance on effectively raising concerns and benefiting from legal whistleblowing protection. This guidance includes informing employees about their rights and signposting the voicing employee to regulators if deemed necessary.[74]

In practice, concerns are usually first raised informally with one's line manager. At the time of our research, the organization was trying to empower line managers to make this pathway more effective. On the other hand, the speak-up policy names the "key persons" as the first point of contact. The first point of contact is responsible for registering the concern, informing the whistleblower that his/her concern is received and logged, identifying a contact person going forward, and arranging an in-person meeting to discuss follow-up activities. The Head of Special Investigations Unit noted:

> *If, for example, as I say, we're interviewing people, first of all, (. . .) we say that they're only being interviewed as a witness, so we would offer the same, whatever information they give to us, you have the same protection as you would under the speak-up policy.*

The key person, in collaboration with the head of HR strategy and planning, determines whether the concern is related to wrongdoing or is a grievance. This is followed by signposting to the relevant function(s), as a speak-up operator notes:

There was a speak-up last year which was, when it originally came in, it was about three-quarters person grievance and one-quarter speak-up. So, again, as the case manager, I had to meet with the individual, talk her through which bits looked like allegations of wrongdoing and which looked like being a personal grievance, and we split it and it went down the two directions.

Concerns about a potential wrongdoing are passed on to the leadership team owner for investigation. Complex cases can be directly referred to the group internal auditor and the head of the special investigations unit. In intricate cases, the investigator sets out terms of reference, which identifies the parties to be involved in the investigation.

Meanwhile, the voicing employee is offered HR support or is signposted to a whistleblowing charity if deemed necessary. A speak-up operator emphasises this aspect as one of the strengths of their current arrangement:

We have a very strong protocol around protecting the individual by checking their comfort levels, (. . .) supporting them. So keeping a very distinct split between the case manager, who typically will probably be someone in HR and the investigator. Having very, very clear divisions of responsibility.

When the investigation is complete, the resulting report is presented to the head of HR strategy and planning and the voicing employee is informed. As can be inferred from this summary, responsiveness is standardized and embedded in the policy document. Speak-up operators communicate with the voicing employee and keep them informed throughout the process. However, a speak-up operator noted during the interview:

We don't necessarily have a touch point three months after the closure and six months after the closure and that's only just occurred to me as I'm speaking. So maybe it's something I need to look at in terms of checking back in.

Speak-up operators try to provide anonymity for the voicing employee but may have to lift it to further the investigation as one of them explains:

If the reporter is required to be involved in the investigation, obviously the anonymity has to be lifted. But we would always lift the anonymity on a very limited basis. So it would be lifted for the investigator and depending on the nature of the complaint.

An HR officer supports this statement:

So my understanding is that they can remain anonymous unless it becomes, I suppose, impossible to investigate it without making you aware of who the individual is.

She also adds that the employee is informed before lifting anonymity:

I know we have had one case where it was alluded there was a speak-up issue attached to it. And we had to—the speak-up operator, I think, was involved—she had to write the individual to say, 'Look, for us to progress this it will involve us passing it over to the work force performance team. Therefore they will know your name . . .'

Risk of retaliation is also addressed in the whistleblowing policy and the voicing employees are assured that they are protected. Nevertheless, the policy notes that a voicing employee may be disciplined if the investigation concludes that his/her claim could not be supported by evidence and was found to be malicious. The head of special investigations says:

I think the bank protects you as much as it can, but at the same time I think under legislation—and I may be wrong here—I don't think there's an overall covering under the legislation. I may be wrong. But the bank, if your claim is not malicious, the bank will protect you against any kind of discipline or anything like that, or any reprisals from senior management, or anybody making—which is a disciplinary action in itself, if people are coming and attacking you, anyway.

We should also note that the speak-up mechanism is designed for, and advertised to, current staff members. If received, concerns from customers and former staff members are also considered but are not recorded as speak-up events. These are subject to a different set of legislation and a separate code of conduct. Thereby, such concerns go through a different procedure.

The person leading the internal investigation states that the average number of cases they deal with at any one time is six and they have handled about sixty cases in the last two years. However, not all of these were classified and recorded as speak-up events. In fact, speak-up events accounted for a fraction of these cases. In the month that preceded our interview, for example, the special investigations unit worked on two speak-up cases. They usually receive less than one per month, and one-third or one-fourth of these do not fall under the category of speak-up as defined by the organization. The speak-up operator expressed his worry about the low number of speak-up calls and mentioned an ongoing debate in the organization about how to interpret it. To inform the debate, they have begun consultations with employees who could potentially refrain from disclosing wrongdoing.

If the take-up is low, the most likely reasons are low levels of trust in the speak-up arrangements or insufficient advertisement. Thereby, the speak-up operator explains, the bank has recently focused their efforts on increasing trust:

> *We have been trying to become, to build a culture which is much more adult-to-adult than the patriarchal culture that used to exist in the classic financial services. So (. . .) our code of conduct (. . .) explicitly calls out, 'If you breach policies, you may be subject to disciplinary procedures up to and including dismissal'. So we tend to be a little bit more black and white where speak-up is concerned.*

Clear communication of policies is important for both creating trust and advertising the speak-up arrangement. At this bank, there are several avenues through which information about speak-up arrangements is disseminated. As mentioned before, the first one is the code of conduct itself, on which all staff is trained. There are about ten compliance and ethics courses that staff members have to complete every year. These courses encourage employees to raise their concerns and provide information about the speak-up channels. Although the organization does not measure the effectiveness of this method, the speak-up operator was able to share some evidence of impact:

> *Just as an anecdote, in our branches our early morning training takes place on a Wednesday and a large proportion of branches (. . .) were doing early morning training last Wednesday morning. And at about ten to ten, when early morning training finishes, my phone rang with one speak-up report and 20 minutes later it rang from somebody else with another speak-up report. Now I hadn't picked it up in the first one but on the second one I said, 'Why did you raise this issue now?' And the guy said, 'We've just done the conflict of interest [compliance and ethics] course and the slide came up and a few of us'—it was this pricing query—'a few of us afterwards were saying, "Maybe that's the way to raise this worry"'.*

In addition to these measures, the top management circulates information emails, which may sometimes provide details about the speak-up arrangements.

Key Learning

This bank shows some of the best practices in speak-up arrangement design and operation.[75]

1. It offers a variety of speak-up channels: the line manager (informal), internally operated hotline, dedicated email account, key persons, and external advice channel. This provides increased accessibility as well as meeting different needs.[76]

2. Different functions are involved in operation of speak-up arrangements with clear protocols. For example, the HR provides necessary support to the voicing employee, while the compliance function carries out the investigation. This prevents speak-up operators from finding themselves in dual dependencies. It also makes best use of each function's expertise.

3. Although the organization has separate arrangements for speak-up, grievance and customer complaints, no concern is turned down for being raised through the wrong channel. Instead, they are signposted to the relevant function.

4. Responsiveness is embedded in the speak-up process and formalised in the speak-up policy.

5. The external advice line gives employees the opportunity to receive support and guidance from an independent body. This not only facilitates effective whistleblowing but also increases trust.

6. All speak-up events are documented.

ENGINEERING

The engineering sector is comprised of many subdisciplines and subsectors including but not limited to: aerospace, civil and environmental, computing and communication, energy and power, manufacturing and design, medical and bioengineering, transport and mechanical.[77] Although engineers do work on public sector contracts, research in the UK, France and Germany shows that the overwhelming majority of engineers (84–91%) work for the private sector.[78] The engineering sector also has major impacts on economies. Based on the employment multiplier effect, it is estimated that every engineer employed creates 1.74 additional jobs.[79] Also, research has shown that there is 'a strong, positive link between engineering strength',[80] gross domestic product (GDP) per capita, and investment per capita. These figures demonstrate the vital role of engineering in economies around the world. Sweden, Denmark and the Netherlands sit at the top of the Engineering Index,[81] while Europe, Asia and Oceania are the best performing geographical regions.[82] In the UK—which currently occupies the fourteenth place in the index[83]—engineering has contributed £486 billion to the GDP (26%) and engineering firms provided 5.7 million jobs (19% of total employment) in 2015.[84]

A report published two years after the 2008 economic crisis showed redundancies, increases in workload, and decreases in wages in the engineering sector as a result of the economic downturn, but recent years have seen some recovery.[85] Figure 3.2 highlights some of the changes that have impacted this area.

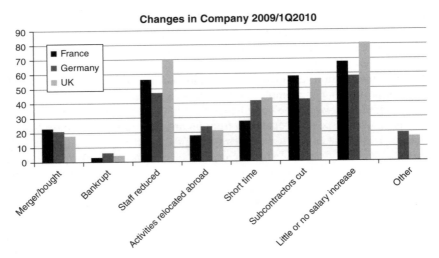

FIGURE 3.2   Chart showing the changes due to economic downturn. *Source:* Adapted from Engineering Council (2010).

Although small firms constitute the majority in the sector (80% of engineering firms in the UK employ only up to four employees), nearly half the engineers work in firms that have at least 250 employees.[86] These larger firms are often multinationals who pose a regulatory challenge as they operate under multiple regulatory regimes, which on the global scale constitute a patchy landscape.[87] This makes the sector particularly vulnerable to various types of wrongdoing.

The most common forms of wrongdoing in the sector include bribery, extortion, fraud, and collusion, which can take place at any point in the life cycle of an engineering project, anywhere from planning to tenders or from execution to maintenance.[88] On top of these, creative accounting and excessive use of derivatives, which have been discussed in the previous section, can also be observed in the sector as was seen in the Enron Scandal[89] As both public and private organizations are often involved in engineering projects, 'any one or more of the government, project owner, funders, consultants, contractors, subcontractors, suppliers, joint venture partners, and agents'[90] may be involved in wrongdoing.

Wrongdoing in engineering firms can cause reputational damage, a decrease in shareholder value, legal liabilities, loss of physical assets (due to collapse, fire, etc.), and even injury or death of employees. It can also damage trust, and decrease demand and investment in the sector. UNESCO notes that 'clients increasingly require assurance that consulting engineering firms operate in a corruption-free environment'[91] because 'competitive bidding on equal terms'[92] is crucial for a free market economy. Yet, it is important to underline that the free market logic is often not the remedy, but the cause of engineering disasters because 'production, schedule, and cost come before investments in comprehensive system safety'[93] when profit-making supersedes all other objectives. The Soma Mine Disaster in western Turkey, where 301 miners died, provides a tragic example to such state of affairs. Their aim of 'maximising production of coal, apparently at the expense of safety',[94] brought about a corrupt production regime that was privatised and deregulated by the government, overlooked by regulators, operated by a company that defied safety standards, and supervised by complicit engineers.[95]

To mitigate wrongdoing that can end in such drastic consequences, some engineers subscribe to an ethical code. In Canada, graduates of engineering programs participate in a ritual that cements the ethics and values of the profession in them, and they receive an iron ring to remind them of their duties (see Box 3.3).

BOX 3.3   THE IRON RING

The Iron Ring is a ring worn by many Canadian-trained engineers, as a symbol and reminder of the obligations and ethics associated with their profession. The ring is presented to graduates in a closed ceremony known as The Ritual of the Calling of an Engineer, developed with the assistance of English poet Rudyard Kipling. The Ritual has a history dating back to 1922, and was begun by a civil engineer, Professor Haultain of the University of Toronto. Haultain felt that an organization was needed to bind all members of the engineering profession in Canada more closely together, and to remind them of their duties and intentions. He also felt that an obligation or statement of ethics to which a young graduate in engineering could subscribe should be developed, so he wrote to Rudyard Kipling, who had made reference to the work of engineers in some of his poems and writings. Haultain asked Kipling for his assistance in developing a suitably dignified obligation and ceremony for its undertaking. Kipling accommodated Haultain and produced both an obligation and a ceremony formally entitled 'The Ritual of the Calling of an Engineer'.

The object of the Ritual is the simple end of directing a newly qualified engineer toward a consciousness of the profession and its social significance and indicating to the more experienced engineer their responsibilities in welcoming and supporting the newer engineers when they are ready to enter the profession.

The Ritual is administered by a body called The Corporation of the Seven Wardens Inc./Société des Sept Gardiens inc. The seven past-presidents of the Engineering Institute of Canada in 1922 were the original seven Wardens. The Corporation is responsible for administering and maintaining the

(Continued)

Ritual and in order to do so creates Camps in various locations in Canada. The Ritual is not connected with any university or any engineering organization; the Corporation is an entirely independent body. The Ritual has been copyrighted in Canada and in the United States. The text of the oath reads:

I, _____, in the presence of these my betters and my equals in my Calling, bind myself upon my Honour and Cold Iron, that, to the best of my knowledge and power, I will not henceforward suffer or pass, or be privy to the passing of, Bad Workmanship or Faulty Material in aught that concerns my works before mankind as an Engineer, or in my dealings with my own Soul before my Maker. My time I will not refuse; my Thought I will not grudge; my Care I will not deny towards the honour, use, stability and perfection of any works to which I may be called to set my hand. My fair wages for that work I will openly take. My Reputation in my Calling I will honourably guard; but, I will in no way go about to compass or wrest judgment or gratification from any one with whom I may deal. And further, I will early and warily strive my uttermost against professional jealousy or the belittling of my working colleagues, in any field of their labour. For my assured failures and derelictions, I ask pardon beforehand, of my betters and my equals in my Calling here assembled; praying, that in the hour of my temptations, weakness and weariness, the memory of this my Obligation and of the company before whom it was entered into, may return to me to aid, comfort, and restrain.[96]

The Iron Ring has been registered and may be worn on the little finger of the working hand by any engineer who has been obligated at an authorized ceremony of the Ritual of the Calling of the Engineer. The ring symbolizes the pride which engineers have in their profession, while simultaneously reminding them of their humility. The ring serves as a reminder to the engineer and others of the engineer's obligation to live by a high standard of professional conduct. It is not a symbol of qualification as an engineer—this is determined by the provincial and territorial licensing bodies.

Adapted from the Ritual of the Calling of the Engineer, Camp One (Toronto) website.[97]

Wrongdoing in the engineering sector can have detrimental effects on the environment, workers' and communities' health and safety, and the economy. Enron's bankruptcy, for example, had a large economic impact as it caused thousands to lose their jobs.[98] But more tragic is the loss of life or the emotional and bodily harm that can result from immediate and/or long-term effects of engineering disasters. In the construction sector, for example, there have been 'building collapses where bribes [were] paid to building inspectors to overlook safety issues [and] have resulted in deaths'.[99] Such wrongdoing can become systemic corruption that encompasses public authorities and the private sector. For example, systemic corruption in Turkey that began with privatisation of land, deregulation of construction, relaxed regulatory oversight, political patronage and capitalist greed in the 1980s has subsequently claimed tens of thousands of lives in 1990s as unlicensed housing developments fell to pieces in successive earthquakes.[100] But even under better health and safety regimes, human mistakes, productivity pressures, understaffing, inadequate infrastructure, insufficient regulation, and lack of effective speak-up arrangements can cause major disasters, such as the Piper Alpha oil rig disaster, which cost 167 lives and $3.4 billion in damages.[101]

Speak-out in the Engineering Sector

Judging by the whistleblowing cases in recent history, we can argue that retaliation against whistleblowers is a common occurrence in the engineering sector.[102] In the last few years, several allegations of victimising employees for externally raising concerns about illegal conduct have been made against engineering firms.[103] The problem was so widespread that researchers have advised engineers to find a new job before blowing the whistle, and discuss their intentions to speak-up with the new employer.[104] As is well known, the prevalence of retaliation creates a culture of silence. IEEE fellow and computer science professor Stephen H. Unger says:

> *I hate the term whistle-blower. It conveys the wrong impression, of someone running around, being noisy and disruptive, behaving in an erratic way. Which is the very opposite of all the engineer whistle-blowers I'm aware of. They did everything they could to avoid publicity, to avoid making waves. Engineers are very quiet people.[105]*

Employees from a variety of sectors face similar circumstances and may be caught between their conscience and the desire to protect themselves from harm when they witness wrongdoing. However, engineers carry a greater responsibility towards the public as the projects they are involved in can cause harm to large numbers of people, animals and the environment.

The first engineering codes of ethics from early twentieth century featured protection of clients' and employers' interests only,[106] leaving out the public interest, workers' health and safety, and protection of the environment. However, the engineering profession's potential to cause harm on a great scale if work is not done properly has led professional bodies and ethicists to include safety, health and welfare of the public among engineers' responsibilities as the profession developed.[107] Today, engineers are often bound by law, professional standards or ethics codes to protect all of these.[108] This means whistleblowing for many is a double-edged sword, in terms of not only the inner conflicts they may experience but also the 'dual dependencies'[109] they may find themselves in. Dual dependencies occur when individuals have simultaneous responsibilities to competing interests. In the example of engineers who witness wrongdoing that they are required by law to report, they may face victimisation for exposing wrongdoing or for being complicit if a colleague breaks the silence, but may also suffer penalties if a catastrophe exposes the truth. Whistleblower protection legislation and effective speak-up arrangements are crucial for engineering-firm employees, especially engineers, in order to prevent appropriate dependencies from being compromised.[110]

One of the earliest and most published examples of a catastrophe in modern engineering history that could have been prevented if effective speak-up arrangements had been in place is the *Challenger* disaster.[111] On 28 January 1986, a space shuttle exploded over Florida, in the United States, seconds after its launch and killed seven crew members.[112] Morton Thiolkol Inc., NASA's subcontractor that manufactured the booster rocket for the *Challenger*, was warned by one of its engineers, Roger Boisjoly, about a potential O-ring failure under cold temperatures six months before the explosion.[113] On the day of the launch, the team of engineers working for the firm tried again to convince their managers to delay due to weather conditions to no avail.[114] In the aftermath, Boisjoly provided his testimony to the Presidential Commission investigating the event and made public the memo in which he alerted his superiors to the risks.[115] Although he had not raised his concerns with the regulators prior to the disaster, he is well known as a whistleblower for exposing how Morton Thiolkol managers neglected health and safety warnings. Although he was later celebrated for his courageous and ethical conduct, he personally paid a very high price. He was isolated by his colleagues and managers, as a result of which his mental and physical health deteriorated to the extent that he could no longer work.[116] His experience exemplifies a failure to investigate concerns, retaliation against and social isolation of voicing employees, all of which are among the primary reasons for the prevalence of a culture of silence and secrecy, as was discussed in the previous section.

Whistleblowing legislation and speak-up arrangements in the engineering sector have been gradually improving since the *Challenger* disaster.[117] This progress is evidenced in some recent victories of whistleblowers in legal battles against retaliation.[118] Implementation of speak-up arrangements, especially hotlines, has steadily increased since 1995 according to Institute of Business Ethics' (IBE) 2016 survey with FTSE 350 companies—among which are engineering firms from mining, oil, industrial, electronic, software, IT, construction and pharmaceutical sectors.[119] The prevalence of speak-up arrangements vary among engineering subsectors, but comprehensive data in this area is not available. We know, for example, that 67% of 163 defence companies from 47 countries have at least one speak-up channel, but only eight of these actively encourage reporting.[120] There are also external reporting systems operated by regulators such as the British Health and Safety Executive (HSE), Civil Aviation Authority (CAA), Maritime and Coastguard Agency (MCA), and Office of Rail and Road (ORR).[121]

Case in Focus

We researched a multinational engineering firm headquartered in Europe that has multiple subsectors including power generation and transmission, transport, and medical imaging. It operates in more than 200 countries and has more than 300,000 employees. It was caught up in a crisis in the mid-2000s when regulators discovered that the company had a slush fund used by managers for bribery purposes. The scandal was extensively covered in the media and court cases were opened in several countries. In a few years, the top management and some middle managers were replaced, and billions were paid in legal settlements. Following the scandal, the company took firm steps towards strengthening its compliance function and creating a speak-up arrangement: an audit organization was created at the group level under the new CEO, a new board position was created, and the specialist compliance function grew tenfold. According to a legal counsel at its headquarters, a speak-up arrangement was implemented as 'an immediate action and reaction to the scandal'.

The arrangement is comprised of a question channel, key internal persons, an external hotline and an external ombudsperson. The question channel was crucial in the initial stages of implementing speak-up arrangements. It helped inform the employees about the channels, explain their purpose and how they work, signpost voicing employees to the right channel or function, and so on. But the need for a question channel has gradually diminished, according to a legal counsel at the headquarters:

> *In the beginning, by building up this [the question channel] offer, it was very important that we have a very quick hotline, a very quick and a very centralized hotline like [the question channel], but the more we are developing our community of compliance, the more the importance of [the question channel] decreases.*

Therefore, a regional compliance officer argues, currently the channel is less frequently used:

> *[The question channel] was more around—you know, [for] general questions. If someone was unsure about something within the compliances, they would use that. But that's less used now. [. . .] The main one is really [the external hotline], just to speak up.*

The external hotline was frequently used to raise concerns from the beginning. The Regional Compliance Officer continues:

> *I think what we've seen is that, in the early days when it first came into being, people were using it for everything. For any sort [of] issues that they had with the company, they would use it which is not what was*

intended. For example, the one I always use is, the car park lights in front of me weren't working one day. Some of the playing real estate department, they never did anything about it so they put it through [the hotline], which clogs up the system. That's one extreme.

This shows that organizational members went through a learning process in which the question channel and the hotline proved very useful. The types of issues one can raise and the channels best suited for the purpose were not immediately clear to the employees. But they collectively learned through these channels.

Concerns about wrongdoing are followed up by the compliance function, and grievances are handled by HR. The two functions work in coordination based on a protocol. All concerns received through available channels are filtered and sign-posted to designated functions. The compliance and HR work together on issues that fall within their remit if a concern has both grievance and wrongdoing components.

The hotline, as a speak-up channel, is specifically for compliance purposes. The regional compliance officer recounts:

I think (. . .) that we had a lot of cases coming through [the hotline], which were more interesting cases, but they very much sat within the HR arena so, you know, bullying, victimization, those types of issues which still need to be looked at, but weren't really anti-corruption, anti-trust, those sort-of pure compliance cases.

The hotline operators use a questionnaire to elicit information that helps categorise the information as grievance or compliance to make necessary referrals. Compliance-related concerns are directed to the central compliance team at the headquarters. They also provide digital chat rooms for anonymous communication between voicing employees and company compliance officers. The legal counsel at the headquarters explains the speak-up process as follows:

The user is guided through all of the process. Employees and external stakeholders can stay anonymous if they want to. We will never obtain any information about their identity if they do not want. Even the [external] provider does not gather such data in accordance with its internal policy to keep the data safely stored without any possibility to access it on their own.

If the operators need to pass on the concern, they inform the voicing employee, tell them to whom the concern will be passed on, and give them the option to opt out. The legal counsel continues:

The reporter also can decide if he or she wants to communicate [directly] with us or not. Therefore, he is able to decide if he wants to create a post-box we can use to safely and anonymously communicate with him. If the whistle-blower decides not to communicate with us anymore after bringing the report to us, this is fine as well. One of the new features is also that there is not a dialogue talking hotline, but a kind of voice intake where reporters can record their message on an automated system.

As he mentions here, the company was 'conducting a trial in a number of countries with a telephone hotline that uses automated voice handling instead of "live" staffed call centre'[122] at the time of our research. But, he also adds that some users were not comfortable with using this new technology:

In the last few months we have learned that for some user groups (...) this new system with an automated in-voice reporting provokes some uneasiness. For [region], we have already changed it. We now have an external call centre especially for [region] where a dialogue with a person at the other end is possible.

While these innovations continue, according to the regional compliance officer, the demand for the hotline is shifting towards key internal persons (local compliance officers and regional managers) and external ombudsperson:

But in terms of usage, I would say, more recently, I've personally seen people perhaps coming more directly to the compliance office or even using the Ombudsman. Not actually using [the hotline], but the procedure. But that's my own personal feeling, where we've seen complaints coming through to my desk.

One could see this shift as a success of the speak-up arrangements in building trust since the shift is from technologically supported anonymous channels to direct communication through informal channels, or, simply as transfer of trust from one channel to another.[123]

The ombudsperson is one of the increasingly popular channels. This channel was also established after the scandal in the first decade of the twenty-first century. The company makes a contract with a lawyer specialising in white-collar crime, economic law or criminal law in general to act as its ombudsperson. They have worked with several different lawyers so far. According to the legal counsel:

The Ombudsman is a communication channel, an objective external channel to report violations, misconduct, et cetera. The investigation, the question how to handle this report, lies with us [the compliance function].

The role of the ombudsperson in the speak-up system is to receive and signpost concerns to the compliance function or the management, to organize follow-up activities, and to facilitate alternative dispute resolution.[124] S/he provides a confidential service to the voicing employee and aspires to neutrality. The legal counsel says:

> *For us, the ombudsman is also very valuable when we need to communicate with the reporter. For example, when the reporter says 'I do not want to bring my identity to the knowledge of [the engineering company], and I want to stay anonymous', then it's his right. The ombudsman only is a channel, as I said, and the ombudsman might know about the reporter's identity. Therefore, we have the possibility to communicate via the ombudsman with a reporter, even if he wants to stay anonymous. (. . .) This is an equal alternative. There is no hierarchy of channels.*

In short, this engineering firm offers a variety of channels by which concerns are received. These filter the concerns about wrongdoing and pass them on to the compliance function. The executive documents and investigates these concerns.[125] The legal counsel explains the process:

> *We have an important tracking tool in which we are tracking all our incoming cases as soon as they are assessed to be compliance cases. Every compliance officer, but my department as well, especially when we have any [hotline] or Ombudsman income—can register cases within this tool. And then every case is permanently assigned an individual number. It is a highly relevant tracking item. When any compliance officer within [the engineering company], for example on local level, receives information about potential misconduct, he is obliged to enter his case—as long as it's a compliance case—in this tool. He can then, in accordance with internal protocols, send it either to us for central handling, or the case can be handled locally. However, every compliance case worldwide is centrally tracked in this tool, both those on local level and on central level. At central, we have the overview over all cases.*

Protocols and procedures were developed in this firm to standardise the follow-up activities. Once the investigation is complete, the person who raised the concern is informed. If they have used an anonymous channel and have not provided contact information, communication can become a problem both during and after the investigation.

The tracking tool mentioned in the preceding excerpt is useful also in collecting and aggregating data. The data collected in this manner is used for pattern recognition, risk analysis, and reporting.[126]

> *The provision of compliance case figures formed part of the company core policy and served the promotion and continuous development of the compliance organization. After the crisis, our own management board*

position for Legal and Compliance was created. (. . .) it was part of his role in the management board to provide the company with all figures regarding compliance, and this includes all relevant factors like speak-up arrangements, and the numbers with regards to investigations and disciplinary measures et cetera. I think, from that intense culture of internal transparency, but as well of pride concerning the effective first steps already taken the motivation arose to put the figures in the annual report. (The legal counsel)

The interviewees asserted that the management and shareholders have been very keen to analyse the speak-up data, which provided internal transparency. The company also provides aggregated figures in its annual report. Although they believe reporting increased investors' and other stakeholders' trust, it has also posed some challenges. Because reporting speak-up data is not yet standardised, their figures have been misinterpreted.[127]

You cannot compare the incoming cases of one period, let's say one year or one quarter, with the disciplinary measures and the closing of the cases, because sometimes complex investigations take more than half a year or more than one year in total. Therefore, the numbers do mostly not refer to the same cases, they are just stating the in- and output of cases without saying anything about how much is still on-going within the compliance organization. If we in one year have an incoming number of 100 cases and disciplinary measures in or closing of 60 cases, that does not mean we are only handling 60 of 100 cases. We may very well have 40 open cases which are passing on to the next quarter or the next year. (The legal counsel)

The company finds it rewarding to report on speak-up data despite some misguided inquiries especially from the media:

By publishing, we promote transparency, demonstrating that the compliance system you've seen is alive and working, and that there are cases being investigated. (The legal counsel)

The speak-up data reveals the uptake of the speak-up arrangement and helps evaluate the behavioural patterns in use of various channels. Reportedly, in the second half of the 2000s after the scandal, a steady increase was observed in speak-up events. The reports reached a peak in the 2010s with 740 compliance-related reports received through the hotline worldwide. This was followed by a steady decrease up until 2015 when 300 speak-up events were recorded. Currently, the numbers seem to be almost constant.

Key Learning

With its experience that spans over a decade, this engineering firm shows some of the best practices in speak-up arrangement design and operation.[128]

1. It offers a variety of speak-up channels: the question channel, the externally operated hotline, internal key persons, and the ombudsperson. Each channel offers a different degree of independence and anonymity, thus meets a different need or attracts a different audience.[129]
2. It involves more than one function in its speak-up arrangements, which liaise through clear protocols. For example, HR and the compliance work together on cases with both grievance and wrongdoing aspects, while all alleged wrongdoing is investigated by the compliance function.
3. Although the organization has separate arrangements for speak-up about wrongdoing and grievance, no concern is turned down for being raised through the wrong channel. Instead, they are signposted to the relevant function.
4. There is evidence of building trust through speak-up arrangements.
5. Responsiveness is formalised through procedures and protocols.
6. There is an effort to standardise and coordinate responsiveness through a global expat strategy.[130]
7. The external hotline and the external ombudsperson make it possible to raise concerns anonymously and provide confidentiality. This encourages employees to speak-up without fear of reprisal.
8. All speak-up events are documented.
9. Speak-up data is used for risk monitoring and published in an annual report.
10. The web-based channel and the hotline are offered in local languages of the regions where they operate. This increases accessibility.

HEALTHCARE

The healthcare sector displays major differences across countries and it is nearly impossible to make meaningful generalisations. Therefore, this introduction will focus exclusively on the UK, where our research was based. In the UK, healthcare provision was nationalised and centralised in 1948 with the formation of the National Health Service (NHS), as part of postwar welfare policies. The ethos of NHS was to provide healthcare universally, free at the point of use. It has been funded from taxes and national insurance contributions by UK residents. It currently serves almost 65 million people and is one of the largest employers in the world with over 1.5 million workers.

As a public institution, the NHS has gone through major reforms in line with government policies and hegemonic ideologies throughout its seven decades of existence.[131] Its current structure has mainly been determined by free-market principles of efficiency, competition and consumerism imposed on the public sector from 1980s onwards.[132] However, the neoliberal one-size-fits-all approach to restructuring the public sector has been criticised for overlooking the peculiarities of healthcare provision, for example, 'the logic of continuity of care rather than one-off choices that infuses some of the best practices in health and social services'.[133]

In 1980s and 1990s, the Department of Health and Social Security (DHSS) introduced 'cost improvement programmes' to extend NHS provisions without extra funding and expected the health authorities to make annual efficiency savings of 0.2% to 0.5%.[134] Trusts were created as more autonomous, local entities in competition with each other. A new funding arrangement in which money followed the patient was introduced assuming 'this would allow purchasers to make better use of the funds available, so as to secure a comprehensive range of high-quality services'.[135] These reforms were followed by the 'patient choice' model introduced in 2002 to increase competition between providers and, subsequently, 'consumer satisfaction'. Underlying all, of course, were the assumptions that: (1) 'consumers' of health care are rational agents capable to make the right choices to meet their healthcare needs; (2) the free market is an inherently efficient mechanism of distributing goods and services.[136] Nevertheless . . .

The evidence on the effects of choice in the 1990s Conservative internal market, in Labour's subsequent choice reforms and in similar reforms in other comparable health systems introduced from the 1990s onwards, suggests at best a very limited impact in terms of efficiency and quality. There are also some indications that the measures intended to promote choice have had a negative impact on equity.[137]

More importantly, in the new consumerist model, quality of care was gradually replaced by consumer satisfaction as the measure of service quality, which resulted in insufficient monitoring and oversight of the quality of care. In the Patient's Charter (1991) that defined the standards of service provided by the NHS, for example, there was no reference to quality of care.[138]

Another systemic problem that reduces the quality of care in the NHS has been underfunded buildings, equipment, and staffing. In the 1980s and 1990s:

Shortages in healthcare professionals, particularly doctors and nurses, to provide the service which was promised were a constant factor. The public came to expect, if not accept, dirty hospitals, poor food, inadequate facilities, long waits, and an uneven quality of care. Healthcare professionals laboured to make ends meet and to care for their patients, working in circumstances which were an affront to the claims made for the NHS.[139]

The NHS, as the biggest healthcare provider and a public sector organization, is of significant concern to the British society since lives and well-being of millions depend on the quality of care it provides. This puts the organization under close scrutiny by the media and the society. A scandal in one trust causes reputational losses to the NHS at a national level. Also, the NHS has always been and continues to be a political battleground. Its success and failures can be put in the service of various political agendas. For some commentators, the imminent danger it faces is to be gradually and purposefully bankrupted by promarket political parties, a common political strategy in (previous) welfare countries that helps legitimise privatisation.[140] Counteracting this process is vital for the NHS at the national level and for individual trusts that crumble under political and financial pressure.

Ultimately, it is UK residents who are at the receiving end of wrongdoing, corruption or systemic failures in the NHS. Losing their lives, health or loved ones due to lack of patient safety, avoiding healthcare services due to lack of trust, and picking up the bill for wasteful practices are some of the ways in which they pay the price. According to a public inquiry in 2001:

> *Around 5% of the 8.5 million patients admitted to hospitals in England and Wales each year experience an adverse event which may be preventable with the exercise of ordinary standards of care. How many of these events lead to death is not known but it may be as high as 25,000 people a year.[141]*

These standards apply to competence of staff, adequate staffing and resourcing, good teamwork and open communication. Effective speak-up systems can play a positive role in preventing wrongdoing and malpractice. They can also create a culture of trust that facilitates better communication and teamwork.

Speak-out in the NHS

Adopting new managerialism was part and parcel of the neoliberal transition in the NHS towards a consumerist model focused on efficiency, throughput and competition.[142] The Griffiths Report, presented to the parliament in 1983, concluded that the NHS must be run like a private organization by hierarchically organized professional managers. Subsequent to acceptance of recommendations in the parliament, the NHS replaced district management team (DMT) structure with general management. The former was based on the principle of 'management by consensus', the latter is a top-down management system.[143] This hierarchical structure, coupled with the complexity the NHS is known for, makes it difficult to navigate the speak-up arrangements.[144]

> *The interdependence of the many different elements of the NHS system adds to the complexity of this issue. Each part of the system has a continuing need for information about what is or may be going wrong and*

indeed on what is going well. The complexity is a potential barrier to important information being received and acted upon in the right places in the system.[145]

Although the NHS is highly regulated, speak-up pathways are not clear, standardised or overseen by a centralised authority.[146] There are several regulators with powers of inspection but coordination among these is reportedly insufficient.[147] There are gaps in follow-up activities including support provision for whistleblowers.[148] The lack of consistency in speak-up policies across NHS organizations as well as insufficient training for speak-up operators and other employees act as a barrier to raising concerns.[149] The NHS is also criticised for its culture 'in which reports of "success" are in constant demand and reports of "failure" are unwelcome'[150] due to fear of reputational damage and its political consequences. Therefore, middle managers often refrain from raising issues to their superiors.[151] This has knock-on effects such as silencing employees with concerns, retaliation against whistleblowers, and lower trust in speak-up arrangements. The Francis Report, a review of speak-up systems in the NHS in which more than 600 individuals from 43 organizations participated, found that:

Only 64% of NHS workers felt confident that their organization would address their concern. Not only do staff feel they are ignored, a significant number fear there will be consequences for them if they do speak up.[152]

Despite these barriers, concerns related to wrongdoing are fairly frequently raised.

Around a third of the staff working in trusts (35.4%, n = 5020) and just under a quarter of the staff from primary care (21.6%, n = 945) reported having raised a concern about 'suspected wrongdoing' in the NHS.[153]

Among trust staff who did not raise a concern, 17.9% cited lack of trust and 14.9% cited fear of retaliation as the reason for not doing so.[154] Among primary-care staff, these figures were 7.5% and 10.4%, respectively. On the other hand, approximately a quarter of all NHS staff reported that they did not know about the speak-up arrangements their organization put in place.[155]

Lack of effective speak-up arrangements in the healthcare sector can cost lives as the paediatric cardiac surgery scandal at Bristol Royal Infirmary (BRI) has shown. Soon after starting to work as a consultant anaesthetist at the paediatric cardiac surgery unit in 1989, Dr. Stephen Bolsin realised that the rates of infant deaths were significantly higher than the national average. In 1990 he wrote a letter to the chief executive of the trust about 'excess deaths'[156] caused by substandard care, but his concerns were dismissed.[157] Dr. Bolsin continued to voice them through different channels. He spoke with his colleagues at the hospital who advised him to collect data that would provide the evidence base for his claims. He spent the next six years following the advice while also raising his concerns with other anaesthetists in Bristol, his hospital peer group from other specialties, the management of the University Hospitals Bristol NHS Foundation Trust (UBHT) and the Department of Health.[158] Unfortunately, none of these channels were effective and no follow-up activities were organized until 1995 either to investigate or to provide him with support.

> *The clinicians in Bristol at least by 1990 had data on their own poor performance relative to that in other centres in the UK which could have caused them at least to pause and reflect. (. . .) An opportunity was not taken in July 1994 by an official of the Department of Health to investigate more closely the outcomes of PCS (paediatric cardiac surgery) in the under 1s. It was only in 1995 that PCS was formally stopped . . . [159]*

The public inquiry has concluded that around one-third of the children who were operated on at the unit received less than adequate care in 1980s and 1990s.[160] As a result:

> *In the period from 1991 to 1995 between 30 and 35 more children under 1 died after open-heart surgery in the Bristol Unit than might be expected had the Unit been typical of other PCS units in England at the time.[161]*

The inquiry also emphasised that substandard care in BRI resulted from a combination of factors including understaffing, the state of buildings and of equipment, deficiency in the performance of staff members, a hierarchical management system which made it difficult to investigate senior members of staff, complexity of the organizational structure, gaps in regulatory oversight, and absence of effective speak-up arrangements.[162]

The paediatric cardiac surgery scandal and similar tragedies (e.g. the Mid Staffordshire scandal) demonstrated the need for effective speak-up arrangements in the NHS to prevent wrongdoing and malpractice. Therefore, the 2000s have seen new governmental and civil initiatives to establish better speak-up arrangements including:

1. Safety Escalation Team (SET): CQC, a prescribed person for the purposes of the 1996 Act,[163] established SET in 2012 to receive and follow-up concerns from NHS, social care workers and members of the public.
2. Monitor: Monitor is the healthcare sector regulator in England and is a prescribed person for the purposes of the 1996 Act.
3. The NHS Trust Development Authority (NHS TDA): NHS TDA is a special health authority supporting NHS trusts in their efforts to obtain foundation trust status. In 2014, it has become a prescribed person for the purposes of the 1996 Act.

4. Professional Regulators: All professional regulators are prescribed persons for the purposes of the 1996 Act.
5. NHS Protect: This is a subdivision of the NHS Business Services Authority overseeing the speak-up arrangement for concerns about fraud, bribery and corruption.
6. Speak-up Charter: Launched by NHS Employers in 2012, the charter encourages organizations to develop their speak-up arrangements.
7. Whistleblowing Helpline: Commissioned by the Department of Health, this is an advice line for healthcare workers. [164]
8. Freedom to Speak Up Guardians: All NHS Trusts have appointed a guardian whose role is to work with Trust leadership to ensure that there are processes in place to facilitate and support staff who want to speak up about issues, and that these processes are effective and continuously improved.
9. National Guardian's Office: The CQC set up this office to assist Guardians in all of the trusts by providing leadership, training and advice for Freedom to Speak Up Guardians. Its role is to also challenge and provide learning and support to the healthcare system as a whole by reviewing trusts' speaking up cultures and the handling of concerns where they have not followed good practice.

While having these speak-up mechanisms is positive in essence, there is a need for addressing gaps, better coordination, clear definition of the remit of each organization and better communication of pathways for raising concerns.[165] It is also important to reach consistency in speak-up arrangements across NHS organizations including trusts in order to prevent problems that employees face when they move from one to another.[166] Research has shown that about 20% of trusts do not have a speak-up policy.[167] Among those who have speak-up policies and procedures, formal and independent channels are a rarity (for example, only 19.5% have a hotline and less than half of these are external).[168] Also, speak-up training is provided only in 57% of trusts to managers and only in 31% of trusts to potential users.[169] These figures suggest that the NHS is still far from best practice in speak-up design.

Case in Focus

We researched a hospital with NHS trust status, located in the Northwest of England. It treats more than 200,000 patients per year and has a workforce of almost 3,000. The trust has had a whistleblowing policy and informal channels at least since the first half of the 2000s. In the early 2010s, it found itself in the middle of a media storm when a number of employees and patients blew the whistle to regulators and the media. Mostly by a former staff member, patient safety concerns were continuously raised to external parties for the next half a decade. The hospital had gone through an internal review process, an invited review process by a royal college, and unannounced inspections by the CQC. At the same time, some staff members were reported to General Medical Council. The trust spent a considerable amount of resources on responding to allegations, while staff morale, especially among middle managers, plummeted.

> *Those guys at one point I think felt quite -the management team in [department] felt quite beleaguered really because obviously we'd had historical whistleblowers (. . .) who didn't use the policy but Public Interest Disclosure process. They and their associates have repeatedly raised concerns with CQC and Monitor, and currently there is one. A concern has been raised again to CQC—same issues, historical stuff but it's by a journalist. Clearly it's a journalist working alongside one of these individuals, at least. So it has felt to them quite relentless, I think, in that team.*

Although the trust believes the allegations were inflated by grievances and to some extent malicious, the management thought the time scales within which they have responded to concerns and their quality of communication was not good enough in these instances. Hence, they decided to review their speak-up arrangements. These reviews coincided with the publication of the Francis Report, which outlined recommendations for NHS organizations. Following these guidelines, the trust implemented new formal speak-up channels including a hotline. The HR director explains the background to reviewing the arrangement as follows:

> *I would say we've really ramped this [the review] up in the last 12 months, and that's partly due to some of the experiences that we've had around the whistleblowing agenda really and partly to do with, because we did see a sort of rise in individuals going externally to CQC as a first port of call, not really talking to anybody internally in a couple of cases.*

Concerned with employers directly voicing their concerns with regulators and the media, the trust introduced a new whistleblowing policy that aims to strengthen its internal speak-up mechanisms. The policy applies to employees who are entitled to 'protected disclosure' under law, while there are other mechanisms such as the complaints policy for patients and other stakeholders. At the time of this research, their arrangement comprised of multiple channels with varying levels of confidentiality, independence and communication interfaces.

The policy sets out a three-channel internal speak-up mechanism and advises the employees to exhaust these channels before externally whistleblowing. The first step identifies line managers and lead clinicians as an informal channel. If the staff feels they can't raise their concerns with these managers or their concerns are not resolved at this level, they are advised to approach an appropriate senior manager (e.g. HR or finance manager) or a manager from another department as a second step. The third step is to approach the trust's senior independent director, who is the whistleblowing champion, if the staff feels previous steps are not effective. The clinical director explains the escalation process as follows:

They [voicing employees] will feel that that issue hasn't been addressed. Now, sometimes they're right. Sometimes it hasn't, in that there's only so many hours in the day. But I think having the escalation process helps bring some focus to those issues, when people feel they haven't been listened to. The sort of issues that get escalated are quite broad issues. An example at the moment is one of our anaesthetists feels that anaesthesia isn't given enough prominence in the hospital. And that's a really broad concept, and in personal discussions, and in written responses to that individual, I've both tried to address the concerns and responded. But even so, there is still a perception on that individual's part that they've still not got special prominence. So that's gone up through the escalation methodology.

In addition to the informal channels, there is an internal hotline, secure 'post boxes' for written concerns, and the option to write a letter directly to the chief executive. Concerns related to fraud, bribery and corruption can be raised directly with the trust's local counter fraud specialist (LCFS) and/or the trust's Director of Finance (DOF), bypassing line management. While formal channels are in place, the HR director believes that 'the culture of [the trust] can be categorized as often being quite an informal one in terms of structures and so on.'[170] The chief executive, for example, has an open-door policy according to the HR director:

She does see a lot of consultants. She receives a lot of emails from consultants, but this [whistleblowing policy] has basically crystallized all of that and put it into a framework.

Although there are designated channels for different types of concerns, voicing employees are not turned down if they chose the wrong pathway. The whistleblowing policy is seen as part of a broader system of voicing and monitoring concerns that includes the complaints policy, the serious incident policy, the grievance policy and more. The HR director explains the approach they try to establish in the organization:

What we're trying to work towards at the moment is not—we don't want to force people down certain routes, but what we've been trying to do over the last few months particularly is just to raise awareness of 'There are a number of ways that and, if you've got a concern, please don't be quiet about it. Please go and speak to somebody.' And there's a whole plethora of ways of doing that. (. . .) Providing people with an outlet—bringing these things out in the open, it doesn't really matter what channel they go through particularly.

All concerns formally raised under the whistleblowing policy are logged, and the follow-up activities and the outcomes are documented in a central repository. When concerns are raised with persons identified in the policy, they are responsible to respond and organize follow-up activities. If concerns are received through the hotline, which is operated by the HR function, they are assessed and reallocated to people who can potentially resolve the matter. Depending on the judgement of the speak-up operator, this may be followed by an informal review, a more formal investigation or an internal inquiry.

Response is formalised in the policy document and includes continuous feedback to the voicing employee until the closure of the case but is subject to usual legal limitations on details of investigations. The clinical director emphasises his efforts to respond in a timely fashion:

I document, and I will basically never leave something like that unanswered because I have to. I know that it's my responsibility as clinical director to respond to those issues, and I try and do it the same day. The more difficult ones are things where there's evidence to be gathered and things like that.

In line with best practice, where possible, voicing employees are included in the process of addressing problems they have identified. The HR director shares an example:

So within that group of people that ultimately, that led the approach to CQC, one of the group, what's the best expression to use for it? Well certainly, he might say he 'outed' himself as the whistleblower because he has said that phrase. Then he could see the Trust board were wanting to do something. He started to work with the Director of [department name] and he's subsequently led the improvement work that's going on.

The hotline makes it possible to raise concerns anonymously or confidentially.[171] However, anonymity may hinder the investigation, act as a barrier to responsiveness or the voicing employee's identity may be guessed by colleagues or those involved in the wrongdoing.[172] The policy explicitly addresses this problem and recommends voicing employees to seek advice if they are concerned about confidentiality. To tackle victimisation, the trust offers emotional and legal support to voicing employees through the Speak-Up Guardian, mentors (for students) and the HR department as well as disciplining those who retaliate. The policy document asserts that the senior independent director, in his/her capacity as the speak-up guardian, should 'check up on the welfare of whistleblowers at mutually agreed regular intervals during and after the process'[173] and that HR will provide information and advice about how to make a protected disclosure.

In addition to these internal mechanisms, the policy document provides information about independent third parties that offer advice to whistleblowers, such as trade unions, regulatory and professional bodies, the NHS and Social Care Whistleblowing Helpline, PCAW, and solicitors. It also lists the external speak-up channels such as SET and Monitor while strongly encouraging staff to exhaust internal mechanisms before external whistleblowing.[174]

The effectiveness of the speak-up arrangement is assessed through periodic audits. If the speak-up operators are found not to comply with the policy, an action plan is implemented by the audit committee. This committee is also responsible for annually reviewing the whistleblowing policy. If necessary, revisions are made in order to reflect changes in speak-up cultures and the most recent developments in whistleblowing legislation.

The HR director is responsible for implementing and disseminating the policy. The staff is informed about the policy primarily through the intranet. They also organized a campaign to advertise the speak-up arrangement as part of which the voicing employees are celebrated and the response they receive is shared. Making the response visible, to the extent that legal regulations allow, is part of the trust's strategy to increase trust and engagement.

The speak-up arrangement is also used as a supplement to existing tools that measure attitudes to patient safety and staff engagement. The HR manager says:

I mean if we saw a pattern of similar kinds of concerns being raised consistently from one particular area of the business, then I think obviously we would intervene at that point.

Although a multiplicity of channels have been in place, concerns have been predominantly raised with line managers and external regulators until the recent campaign. According to the HR director, the formal policy has been invoked once or twice in the year preceding the policy review that introduced a hotline. However, the clinical director receives multiple concerns on a daily basis:

Basically, every day I have probably between five and ten interactions that could be described as a whistle-blowing disclosure to me, in that whenever anybody raises a concern to do with service provision or performance or any aspect of that, that is a disclosure as far as I'm concerned. And it's my ability to respond to those things which stops any higher process being invoked.

Key Learning

Having taken lessons from the build-up to the scandal, this NHS trust displays some of the best practices in speak-up arrangement design and operation.[175]

1. It offers a variety of speak-up channels: Informal channels (line managers and lead clinicians), the question channel, key internal persons (the whistleblowing champion, the HR director), an internal hotline and external independent advice (trade unions, regulatory and professional bodies, the NHS and Social Care Whistleblowing Helpline, PCAW). Although greater emphasis is put on informal channels in the policy, and these are more popular among staff, channels with varying degrees of formality, independence and anonymity are available.
2. It involves more than one function in its speak-up arrangements. Whereas the HR and the board focus mainly on employment and patient safety issues, the trust local counter fraud specialist and the finance department respond to concerns about fraud, bribery, and corruption.
3. Speak-up data is used to increase trust in the speak-up arrangement.
4. Although the trust has separate arrangements for speak-up for patient-safety issues, grievances, and wrongdoing, no concern is turned down for being raised through the wrong channel. Instead, they are redirected to the designated channel.
5. Responsiveness is formalised through the whistleblowing policy.
6. There is awareness of the barriers to responsiveness such as anonymity and legal limitations and strategies are developed to circumvent them.
7. The trust works towards standardising and coordinating responsiveness across management. The policy registers managers' duties to respond promptly and appropriately.
8. The whistleblowing resource on the intranet provides information about the types of support offered by and ways to contact independent third parties.
9. Speak-up events received through the formal channels are registered in a central repository.
10. The speak-up data is used to monitor attitudes to patient safety and staff engagement.

CONCLUSION

In this chapter, we have analysed speak-up arrangements in organizations from banking, engineering, and healthcare sectors against the sectoral, economic and political backdrop. There are both parallels and differences in their speak-up cultures and mechanisms because each has a particular history of whistleblowing, different concerns raised through speak-up channels and distinct needs. In all three organizations we studied, speak-up arrangements were implemented in response to a crisis as managers sought to repair the reputational damage, increase employers', investors' and clients' trust, and prevent similar events from recurring. They also all had an organizational culture of silence and complicity, resulting from different sectoral features, which speak-up arrangements have helped change. At the time of the research, they all offered multiple speak-up channels with various degrees of independence, anonymity and formality. These arrangements evolved through time as speak-up cultures and legislation changed. In Chapter 5 we discuss key learnings from this study in an attempt to distill best practice in speak up arrangements.

As our research shows, however, effective policies and arrangements to enable employees to speak up are not sufficient to combat malpractice. In each sector, types of wrongdoing or malpractice that necessitate speak-up are different. Generally speaking, these are: creative accounting, financial engineering and tax avoidance in the banking sector; health and safety, protection of the environment, corruption, and creative accounting in the engineering sector; patient safety, health and safety, and corruption in the health sector. The differences result from their fields of operation (banks trade in financial assets, engineering firms build the material environment, healthcare providers work with vulnerable people) and their positioning in respect to the public-private sector divide (the banking sector is mostly private and deregulated, engineering firms are often commissioned by public authorities, healthcare organizations—at least in the UK—are heavily regulated and under constant political pressure).

Organizational structures can create barriers to speaking up. Banks are hierarchical and the sales department is typically higher in the hierarchy than the compliance function. It is difficult to monitor and sanction wrongdoing or unethical conduct in the sales department as they frequently engage in risky practices but are positioned above compliance. In the engineering sector, engineers are in a position to identify and speak-up against wrongdoing but the final decisions lie with managers whose primary concern is often profit-making, not health and safety. The NHS is complex and hierarchical, while speak-up pathways are unclear and regulators are not well-coordinated, making it difficult to navigate speak-up channels. It is also important to note that these structures are affected by organizational ethos. Sales-oriented banking strengthened the position of the sales department at the expense of compliance, while market-oriented policies in the NHS created a shift in focus from patient safety to patient satisfaction, which resulted in exclusion of the former from quality of care assessments. The engineering sector, however, provides a positive example as its codes of ethics have been expanded in the last few decades to include public interest, workers' health and safety, and protection of the environment among engineer's responsibilities.

Organizations are embedded in and partly determined by social, economic and political structures. Thereby, it is important to acknowledge that the root causes of problems raised through speak-up arrangements are often systemic. The cases we have discussed in this chapter show the impact of deregulation, globalisation, privatisation, and austerity on the structure, ethos, culture and management of organizations. Although speak-up arrangements help prevent wrongdoing and malpractice on a case-by-case basis, a more structural change is often needed. In order to affect structural change, organizations can inform policy debates and public opinion by registering, analysing and reporting on speak-up data.

ENDNOTES

1. Miceli and Near (1985: 4).
2. However, the statutory definition of whistleblowing in the UK and elsewhere is more limited in its scope as it excludes those who does not fall under the legal category of 'worker', such as volunteers and nurses in training in the NHS (Lewis et al., 2015: 312).
3. As will be discussed in the next section, in accounting, for example, this grey area becomes larger.
4. Greenwood (2015: 490).
5. Also see Weiskopf and Tobias-Miersch (2016: 622).
6. Francis (2015: 9).
7. IBE (2014: 4).
8. IBE (2016: 3).
9. IBE (2016: 3).
10. For a full outline of our empirical project methodology, see appendix.
11. IBE (2016: 29–30).
12. Kenny (2014); Kenny (2019).
13. Greenwood and Scharfstein (2013: 3).
14. Partnoy (2006); Sherman (2009); Angelides et al. (2011); Nyberg (2011).
15. Sherman (2009: 11).
16. Sherman (2009: 11).
17. Kenny (2014), (2019); Nyberg (2011: 31).
18. Kenny (2014: 8–9).
19. Sherman (2009: 11); Kenny (2014: 14); Angelides et al. (2011: xviii); Nyberg (2011).
20. Véron et al. (2004: 81).
21. Ibid.: 82.
22. Ibid.
23. See Véron et al. (2004: 42).
24. Ibid.: 29–30.
25. Partnoy (2006: 54).
26. Ibid.: 56.
27. Véron et al. (2004: 25).
28. Ibid.: 26–27.
29. Ibid.: 29–30.
30. House of Representatives (2008).
31. Kenny (2014).

32. Nyberg (2011: 50).
33. FDIC (2017).
34. Ibid.
35. Also see Labaton Sucharow (2012).
36. O'Grady (2010).
37. Wayne et al. (2014).
38. For example see Nyberg (2011); Angelides (2011); Vandekerckhove, Fotaki, Kenny, Humantito, and Ozdemir Kaya (2016); U.S. SEC (2013).
39. Tenbrunsel and Thomas (2015: 9).
40. Kenny (2014: 5); Tenbrunsel and Thomas (2015: 2).
41. See also Heffernan (2012).
42. Kenny (2014: 17).
43. Ibid.: 17.
44. Kenny (2014: 23); Nyberg (2011: 91); Angelides et al. (2011: 12).
45. Kenny (2014: 27–28).
46. These attitudes exemplify two types of logical fallacies categorized under *ad hominem*, that is, poisining the well and appeal to motive. As such, they reveal efforts to dodge allegations by attacking the person who has made them.
47. Kenny (2019).
48. PCAW (2016: 8–9).
49. Ibid.: 9.
50. Labaton Sucharow (2012: 6).
51. Kenny (2014); Nyberg (2011: iii).
52. Sherman (2009:11); Kenny (2014: 14); Cornford (2009: 3); Angelides et al. (2011: xviii); Nyberg (2011).
53. Nyberg (2011: 8).
54. Kenny (2014); Nyberg (2011: iii).
55. Marks (2016); Tenbrunsel and Thomas (2015: 2).
56. Stothard and Buck (2015).
57. Garside (2015); Hamilton (2015); Stothard and Buck (2015).
58. Garside (2015); Hamilton (2015); Stothard and Buck (2015).
59. Garside (2015).
60. Ting (2014); Robinson (2015); Marks (2016).
61. Robinson (2015).
62. WIN (2016). Comp: Please carry queries throughout: AU: in note 65, please provide reference for BBC 2016
63. BBC (2018).
64. BBC (2016).
65. Marks (2016).
66. Ibid.
67. FCA (2015b).
68. PCAW (2016: 8).
69. Ibid.
70. Ibid.
71. U.S. SEC (2013: 8).
72. Ibid.

73. Buy-to-let properties are homes that the owner purchases with the intent that they will be let out to tenants. The risk in these properties is if tenants don't move in, the owner may not be able to afford the mortgage, as they may have a mortgage already on the home that they actually live in.

74. For a detailed discussion on these channels see Vandekerckhove, Fotaki, Kenny, Humantito, and Ozdemir Kaya (2016: 10).

75. For a detailed discussion see Vandekerckhove, Fotaki, Kenny, Humantito, and Ozdemir Kaya (2016b).

76. Vandekerckhove, Fotaki, Kenny, Humantito, and Ozdemir Kaya (2016b).

77. Cebr (2016: 4).

78. The Engineering Council (2010: 3).

79. Mellors-Bourne et al. (2017: ii).

80. Cebr (2016: 2).

81. Calculated on the basis of exports, business, infrastructure, wages, etc. in the sector, the Engineering Index evaluates performance of national engineering sectors (Cebr, 2016: 1).

82. Cebr (2016: 1).

83. Ibid.

84. Mellors-Bourne et al. (2017).

85. The Engineering Council (2010: 7).

86. Mellors-Bourne et al. (2017: vii).

87. Cornford (2006: 36).

88. Stansbury and Stansbury (2010: 193).

89. Partnoy (2006).

90. Ibid.: 193.

91. Boswell (2020: 195).

92. Ibid.

93. Wilcutt and Whitmeyer (2013: 4).

94. Human Rights Watch (2015).

95. Ibid.

96. Blogspot (2015).

97. Camp One (2017).

98. Jopson (2006).

99. Stansbury and Stansbury (2010: 191).

100. Green (2005).

101. Wilcutt and Whitmeyer (2013).

102. Fitzgerald (1990); Oliver (2003).

103. For example see Neate (2014); Smith (2016).

104. Oliver (2003: 253).

105. Kumagai (2004).

106. Petersen and Farrell (1986: 8).

107. Petersen and Farrell (1986: 9).

108. Oliver (2003: 248).

109. Kenny (2014: 8).

110. Ibid.

111. Martin (2012); Fitzgerald (1990); Weil (n.d.); Oliver (2003).

112. Martin (2012).

113. Ibid.
114. Ibid.
115. Martin (2012); Fitzgerald (1990).
116. Martin (2012); Fitzgerald (1990).
117. Oliver (2003); Kumagai (2004); Vandekerckhove, Fotaki, Kenny, Humantito, and Ozdemir Kaya (2016); IBE (2016).
118. For example, see Odell (2013).
119. Donde (2016: 33).
120. Fish et al. (2015).
121. Engineering Council (2015).
122. Vandekerckhove, Fotaki, Kenny, and Humantito (2016: 12).
123. Also see ibid.: 13.
124. Ibid.: 11.
125. For a longer discussion about practices and procedures of recording voice events at the firm, see Vandekerckhove, Fotaki, Kenny, and Humantito (2016: 16).
126. Ibid.: 21.
127. Ibid.: 22.
128. For a detailed discussion see Vandekerckhove, Fotaki, Kenny, and Humantito (2016).
129. Ibid.
130. See Vandekerckhove, Fotaki, Kenny, and Humantito (2016: 24).
131. Kennedy et al. (2001: 50).
132. Fotaki (2016); Kennedy et al. (2001).
133. Fotaki (2016: 3).
134. Kennedy et al. (2001: 51).
135. Ibid.: 54.
136. Fotaki (2016).
137. Fotaki (2014: 7).
138. Kennedy et al. (2001: 56).
139. Ibid.: 58.
140. Cohn (1997: 586).
141. Kennedy et al. (2001: 16).
142. Kennedy et al, (2001: 5).
143. Kennedy et al. (2001: 52).
144. Lewis et al. (2015: 314); Francis (2015: 30).
145. Francis (2015: 30).
146. Ibid.: 89.
147. Francis, (2015: 89).
148. Kennedy et al. (2001: 78).
149. Francis (2015: 89).
150. Ibid.: 9, 30.
151. Ibid.: 120.
152. Ibid.: 34.
153. Ibid.: 214.
154. Ibid.: 214
155. Ibid.: 214
156. Ibid.: 4–5.
157. Ibid.: 161.

158. Ibid.: 161.
159. Kennedy et al. (2001: 9); *The Telegraph* (2001).
160. Kennedy et al. (2001: 2).
161. Ibid.: 2.
162. Ibid.
163. Short for the Employment Rights Act 1996, which regulates a worker's right not to be subjected to any detriment by his employer for making a protected disclosure to prescribed persons.
164. For a full list and more detail see Francis (2015: 44–49).
165. Francis (2015: 49).
166. Ibid.: 49.
167. Lewis et al. (2015: 315).
168. Ibid.: 315–316.
169. Ibid.: 323.
170. Excerpt from an interview with the HR director.
171. Confidentiality differs from anonymity in that the voicing employee's identity is known to the speak-up operator on condition that it is not revealed to third parties without his/her explicit consent.
172. Vandekerckhove et al. (2016: 18); The Trust Whistleblowing Policy Document.
173. The Trust Whistleblowing Policy Document.
174. See the previous section for a more comprehensive list.
175. For a detailed discussion see Vandekerckhove et al. (2017).

CHAPTER 4

Challenges and Obstacles to Effective Speak-up Arrangements

In the previous chapter, we used empirical research to highlight some of the best practices that organizations use to implement speak-up arrangements. The organizations were from various sectors, and had some similarities and some differences in how they approached this. It emerged from these findings that effective speak-up processes are a collective endeavor, requiring support for employees that want to speak up and an organizational culture that is conducive to such reports. In this chapter, we discuss how people speak up, and what some of the barriers to speak-up arrangements are.

In the previous chapter we showed how the organizations we studied used combinations of speak-up channels with different interfaces. In this chapter we discuss the challenges and obstacles faced by those who operated these speak-up arrangements. We first present research findings on how people speak-up and how many times they do so. Next, we discuss what people who speak up expect from those they address their concern to. We then switch perspectives to those who must meet the expectations of whistleblowers—who receive their concerns and operate speak-up arrangements—and delve into the challenges of obtaining and maintaining trust throughout the process. Toward the end of the chapter we introduce our model for developing sustainable speak up systems, which draws on these empirical insights along with best practice from existing research.

HOW DO PEOPLE SPEAK UP?

As discussed in Chapter 2, research into who whistleblowers turn to with their concerns has predominantly used an internal/external dichotomy with little or no differentiation within these categories. One exception is the study by Kaptein,[1] which measured the impact of organizational culture on how people raise a concern about wrongdoing, differentiating between inaction, confronting the wrongdoer, reporting to management, calling an internal hotline, and external whistleblowing. Kaptein's Corporate Ethical Virtue model (CEV model) covers seven aspects that encourage 'ethical conduct'—structures, policies and behaviours that stimulate organization members to behave in an ethical manner. The CEV model articulates these aspects as seven organizational virtues: clarity, congruency, feasibility, supportability, transparency, discussability and sanctionability.

Clarity refers to the extent that organizations reduce vagueness and ambiguity about what is expected behaviour. The more employees are left to their own intuition, the less clear the organization is, and the higher the risk of unethical conduct.

Congruency refers to the extent that management behaviour is in line with the expectations formulated towards employees—in other words, management by example. In a study using the CEV model for researching whistleblowing, Kaptein[2] distinguished between congruency of local management and senior management. In the context of whistleblowing, this is an obvious distinction. Whistleblowing cases often involve an employee reporting perceived misconduct by local management to senior management. What Kaptein[3] wanted to find out was to whom employees were more likely to report depending on how local and senior management scored on congruency. If local management scored low on value congruency but senior management scored high, one would expect employees to report to senior management. But if both scored low, would employees be more likely to blow the whistle outside of their organization or would they prefer to remain silent?

The organizational virtue of *feasibility* refers to how employees feel enabled to fulfil their responsibilities through the provision of time, budgets, equipment, information, etc. *Supportability* refers to the extent to which organizations stimulate employees' identification with the ethics of the organization. It does not measure commitment to the organization, but only the extent to which they support the ethics of the organization, for example through codes of conduct and ethics training. The underlying proposition is that a high level of identification with the ethics of the organization will result in an intrinsic motivation to comply with the ethical standards of the organization.

Another dimension of ethical culture is *transparency*. More precisely internal transparency as the extent to which wrongdoing and its impact would be easily visible to members of the organization—those who could raise concern about it as well as those who can act upon it internally, both employees and managers.

The virtue of *discussability* refers to the extent to which ethical dilemmas or concerns can be discussed internally. Organizations that have a 'code of silence' would score very low on this. The proposition here is that in organizations with low discussability, speaking up is perceived as undesirable, and more effort will be put into retaliating against the messenger than into resolving the malpractice. Finally, the organizational virtue of *sanctionability* refers to the extent to which unethical behaviour is negatively sanctioned and ethical behaviour is positively sanctioned.

Kaptein[4] used this CEV model to see whether these organizational virtues stimulating ethical conduct would make a difference on what individuals intended to do if they saw misconduct in their workplace. Would they remain silent? Would they raise it directly with the wrongdoer? With their manager? Would they call the hotline, or go to top management? Or would they skip all internal routes and blow the whistle outside at once? (See Box 4.1.)

BOX 4.1   KAPTEIN'S RESEARCH ON CULTURE AND ETHICAL BEHAVIOUR

This study focused on the impact of organizational culture on how people raise a concern about wrongdoing, differentiating between inaction, confronting the wrongdoer, reporting to management, calling an internal hotline, and external whistleblowing. The study provides insights into how organizational context such as: management congruency, feasibility of tasks and internal transparency supports employees to trust some potential recipients more than others. For example, if management is perceived as behaving according to the values they espouse (congruency), employees stated a higher intention to whistleblow to them compared to remaining silent or blowing the whistle externally. In contrast, in a context of high internal transparency, employees stated a higher intention to either remain silent or blow the whistle externally. Kaptein's study however does not include a measurement of how people continue to raise their concerns—and does not for instance consider how organizational culture influences whether one would raise a concern after confronting the wrongdoer, or after reporting it to the management.

The study included respondents from organizations that employ over 200 people: 28% of the respondents worked for an organization of 200–1,000 employees, 15% of 1,000–3,000 employees, 9% of 3,000–5,000 employees, 11% of 5,000–10,000 employees, and 38% of more than 10,000 employees.[5]

The industries that the respondents worked in were: Consumer Markets (16%), Government and Public Sector (14%), Healthcare (9%), Automotive (8%), Aerospace/Defense (7%), Electronics/Software (7%), Banking and

(Continued)

TABLE 4.1   Kaptein's Findings

	Inaction	Confront	Reporting to Management	Hotline	External
Clarity	−	+	+	+	−
Congruency Local Management		−	+	−	−
Congruency Senior Management		−		+	+
Feasibility				+	+
Supportability	−	+	+	+	
Transparency	+	−	−		+
Discussability	−	+	+	−	−
Sanctionability	−	+	+	+	−

Source: Adapted from Kaptein (2011c).

Finance (7%), Pharmaceuticals (7%), Media and Communications (6%), Insurance (6%), Chemicals and Diversified Industrials (5%), Power and Utilities (4%), Real Estate/Construction (2%), Forestry/Mining (1%), and Oil and Gas (1%).[6]

The findings are interesting because they point out that organizations cannot simply rely on great cultures to make internal whistleblowing work. Most, but not all, aspects of the CEV model point to employee preferences not to remain silent, and not to blow the whistle outside. Clarity, discussability, and sanctionability do what we expect them to do. The clearer tasks and responsibilities are within an organization, the more employees are willing to confront a perceived wrongdoer directly or raise the concern with management, and the less likely it is they will remain silent or blow the whistle outside of the organization. The same goes for organizations in which employees feel concerns are discussed openly, and management is seen to sanction wrongdoers. Also, the more an organization tries to get its employees to identify with the official ethical standards, the more they are likely to discuss issues openly or raise them with management. They are also less likely to remain silent. However, an interesting finding is that supportability does not seem to have an impact on external whistleblowing. People are just as likely to go outside, whether you have ethics trainings and codes in place or not. These findings are illustrated in Table 4.1.

Other unexpected findings relate to the organizational virtues of congruency, feasibility, and transparency. Kaptein[7] found that a high level of congruency—when management is seen to act according to the ethical standards they preach—indicates that employees are less likely to discuss a concern directly with the wrongdoer. A suggested reason for this is that employees who see their management as behaving with integrity will regard them as role models. Hence, they will expect management to step in rather than directly confront wrongdoers themselves. An odd finding that complicates matters somewhat is that a high level of congruency of senior management did not lead to an intention to report concerns to senior management. Rather, it makes it more likely the employee will either use the internal hotline, or actually blow the whistle outside of the organization.

We can see this too where organizations score high on feasibility. Employees that have all the resources they require to do their jobs express more intention to blow the whistle externally. And in organizations that have a lot of internal transparency, employees express less intention to directly confront a wrongdoer or report to manager. It seems they are more likely to either remain silent or blow the whistle outside. There is a similar rationale to this. A lot of internal transparency means everyone knows who decides what, and where what happens comes from. Hence, if anyone notices any wrongdoing, then surely all the others—including management—can see it happening too. Rather than feeling an urge of responsibility, employees start wondering why no one else is raising this. Thus, they either remain silent or blow the whistle outside.

Kaptein's research shows that even ethical organizations need whistleblowing policies, precisely because some of their ethical virtues will lead employees either to remain silent—potentially losing their commitment—or to blow the whistle outside. Kaptein's findings do not suggest organizations should neglect congruency, feasibility or internal transparency; these are very important virtues to work on in an organization. What they do suggest is that high levels of these virtues will not lead employees automatically to either discuss their concerns openly or raise them with management. A speak-up arrangement can compensate for this. It can help things go right even when something goes wrong. It is both interesting and important to consider Kaptein's insights alongside practical research into the implementation of speak-up systems, including empirical work being carried out in Australia.[8] Based on research into public sector organizations, the authors outline the elements of an organizational whistleblowing programme that, they note, are required to enhance a culture of supportiveness for speaking up. These include: organizational commitment, encouragement of reporting, assessment and investigation of reports, internal witness support and protection and an integrated organizational approach. The authors describe some examples of an integrated approach to embedding the programme in everyday actions as:

- Explicit observations by management that reporting wrongdoing is in line with the organiztion's ethical culture (as expressed in the code of conduct or equivalent mechanism), as well as being in accordance with the expectations of government and the public interest.

- All levels of management setting a personal example by supporting staff who come forward with reports of wrongdoing and 'owning' the report.
- With their consent, publicly acknowledging particular staff who have come forward with reports of wrongdoing.
- Building an understanding of whistleblowing processes through formal training mechanisms.
- Linking the treatment of staff who come forward with reports of wrongdoings to the assessment of the competence of managers.

  (From Roberts et al., 2011: p. 101)

In assessing best practice for developing supportive cultures in the implementation of speak-up systems therefore, it is useful to consider best practice from research alongside empirical evidence.

WHISTLEBLOWING IS A PROTRACTED PROCESS

In the previous section we argued that it is important to distinguish between different internal speak-up recipients. We used the research by Muel Kaptein that shows strong cultures do not automatically lead to effective informal speak-up practices. Kaptein's research however does not consider the possibility of speaking up to different recipients in a sequence. The study does not include a measurement of how people continue to raise the concern—for example how one would raise a concern after confronting the wrongdoer, or after reporting to management. As briefly discussed in Chapter 2, there is a growing body of research showing whistleblowing is a protracted process, in which concerns about 'mistakes' can escalate to complaints and accusations, if not handled well. This research suggests whistleblowing is a process of both real and anticipated responses to the raising of a concern, rather than a one-off decision.

Skivenes and Trygstad[9] researched whistleblowing in the Norwegian public sector, and distinguish between weak, strong internal and strong external whistleblowing. The notion of strong whistleblowing puts an emphasis on process, as Skivenes and Trygstad define it as:

> *Where there is no improvement in, explanation for, or clarification of the reported misconduct from those who can do something about it. In such cases, an employee must report the misconduct again and is thus engaging in strong whistleblowing.*[10]

The study found that 36% engaged in strong whistleblowing, with 29% raising the concern four times. The study however does not provide findings for specific internal and external recipients. Lewis and Vandekerckhove[11] used data from a survey of NHS Trusts in the UK, showing that internally more than half of the

Trust employees raise their concern first with their line manager either informally (52.3%) or in writing (7.3%). The first external recipient of concerns is their trade union (38%), followed closely by professional body (35%). The study does not give further specification about internal or external paths. However, it does show that those who followed their organization's whistleblowing procedure were more likely to proceed to raise their concern externally when internal recipients showed to be ineffective or resulted in retaliation.

Interviewing more than 200 whistleblowers in the United States, Rothschild and Miethe[12] find that '[many] came to their whistle-blowing almost by accident'.[13] Employees raised their concern with their line manager and then further with senior management, each time believing the recipient would step in to correct the situation. Only after voicing their concern internally twice did they consider going to authorities outside the organization. By that time, their initial concern had become compounded with frustration and allegations of retaliation. One of the most important findings of their research is that:

> *[it] is management's response that shapes the potential whistle-blower's subsequent actions. Specifically, our interviews revealed a common pattern in which management's efforts to discredit or retaliate against the claimant become the major catalyst for the political transformation of the concerned employee into a 'persistent resister'.[14]*

In an attempt to track reporting paths whistleblowers take, Donkin et al.[15] used data from two surveys of Australian public sector workers. Unfortunately the two surveys differ in the way they captured the sequence of reporting. One survey asked respondents to indicate with whom they raised their concern the first time, second time, and so on. The other survey asked respondents to indicate with whom they raised first, and list all subsequent recipients without indicating the sequence. Findings show that 97% of whistleblowing starts as internal speak-up, and 90% remains internal. It is also clear that line managers and senior management are generally the first two ports of call.[16]

Research in the UK based on data from an advice line for whistleblowers[17] allows more insight into how a whistleblowing process unfolds. For 868 cases, the research traced what the initial and subsequent three attempts to raise a concern looked like, that is, to who did the employee speak-up the first four times. In the 868 cases a concern had been raised at least once, in 484 at least twice, in 142 at least three times, and in 22 cases the concern had been raised four times. Table 4.2 gives an overview of the protractedness of the whistleblowing cases.

Hence, in 54.8% of the cases, whistleblowers will speak up more than once. The research also found that not only do whistleblowers raise their concern internally before they do so externally, but they tend to raise internally more than once before going external, if they go external at all. Table 4.3 gives an overview of

TABLE 4.2 Number of times a whistleblower raises the concern ($n = 868$).

No. of Times Concern Is Raised	n (%)
One	384 (44.2%)
Two	342 (39.5%)
Three	120 (13.8%)
Four	22 (2.5%)

Source: Based on data from Vandekerckhove, James, and West (2013).

TABLE 4.3 Internal and external whistleblowing.

	Internal	External	Union	Total
First attempt	778 (89.6%)	75 (8.6%)	15 (1.7%)	868 (100.0%)
Second attempt	350 (72.3%)	115 (23.8%)	19 (3.9%)	484 (100.0%)
Third attempt	85 (59.9%)	51 (35.9%)	6 (4.2%)	142 (100.0%)
Fourth attempt	10 (45.5%)	11 (50.0%)	1 (4.5%)	22 (100.0%)

Source: Adapted from Vandekerckhove, James, and West (2013).

internal, external, and union recipients in the whistleblowing process excluding 'other'.

In the PCAW sample of 868 cases, a concern was raised 1516 times, 80.7% of which was internal, 16.6% external, and 2.7% to a union representative. Whilst the number of those making external disclosures increases as the whistleblowing process becomes more protracted, it never surpasses the number of those making internal disclosures.

Who are the recipients of speak-ups? Figure 4.1 shows whom whistleblowers raised their concern with at each attempt. Donkin et al.[18] found in their Australian field study that line managers and higher management were by far the most used 'ports of call' for whistleblowers. Table 4.2 shows that the UK field study confirms this. Unlike Donkin et al[19] however, the UK data allows to give a more detailed picture of who the recipients are. Only 7% raised their concern initially directly with the wrongdoer, whilst more than half of the whistleblowers in the sample (52%) first raised their concern with their line manager. More than one in five (22%) do so with higher management in the first instance but a higher proportion (33%) goes to higher management when raising their concern a second time. Other recipients showing an increase at the second instance are specialist channels, regulators, external bodies, and grievances. Their usage increases even more at the third instance. We also need to note that by the third and fourth attempt whistleblowers are most likely to pursue the matter via a grievance procedure. It must

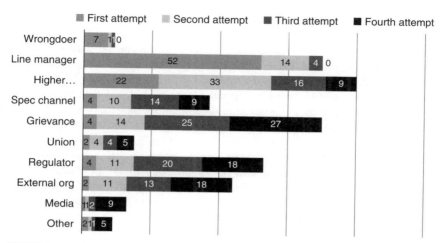

FIGURE 4.1   Frequency series of recipients per attempt (in rounded percentages, $n =$ 868). *Source*: Based on data from Vandekerckhove, James, and West (2013).

be noted that a grievance procedure is unsuited to a whistleblowing concern. A grievance procedure is a complaint procedure, and hence places the onus on the individual to prove the complaint. A whistleblower however is a witness, passing on information to those with a responsibility to address the problem. A witness should not have to prove their concern.

Many would argue that raising a concern with the wrongdoer directly or with your line manager cannot be called internal whistleblowing because the concern is not raised outside of the hierarchical line. However, Rothschild and Miethe[20] highlight that it is the response from that line manager that makes someone a whistleblower. It might very well be that those who first raise concerns with the line managers do not perceive themselves as whistleblowers, at least not at that time. The responses they get from the wrongdoer or their line managers, however, might lead them to identify as whistleblowers. In other words, people tend to approach higher management the second time they attempt to speak out, while it is common to seek out a specialist channel, regulator, or an external body in both the second and third instance. This suggests that whistleblowers seek to raise their concern with increasingly independent recipients, rather than merely deciding to blow the whistle externally if an internal channel is unsuccessful as is often thought.

The PCAW research also highlights patterns within the sequences of recipients used by whistleblowers to raise a concern.[21] For whistleblowing where a specialist channel (compliance, auditor, HR) was the final recipient and was also the second attempt, 56% of the previous reports were to the line manager and 24% were raised with higher management. Where the sequence involved three attempts, the salient pattern was as follows: first line manager, then higher manager, and then specialist channel (55%). This finding has an important implication for organizational actors operating such a specialist channel—e.g. audit, compliance, HR. These channels are often named in organizational whistleblowing or speak-up policies, and nearly always guarantee whistleblowers that their identity will be kept confidential. Both the PCAW[22] data from the UK as well as Donkin et al.'s[23] Australian data suggests that the vast majority of those using a specialist channel have already raised their concern with someone else before using the specialist channel. The implication is that in most cases, either the whistleblower's line manager, higher management, or both know who has raised the concern that auditors or compliance officers might investigate. Specialist channels as recipients of whistleblower concerns might act wisely to make whistleblowers aware of this risk, and in any case carry out investigations assuming others will know who the whistleblower is.

Other patterns also underline the significant role of management's responsiveness.[24] Where the whistleblowing process ended with a regulator, salient sequences also involved line managers and higher management. For sequences of two attempts, these were as follows: line manager before regulator (56%), and higher management before regulator (25%). For sequences of three attempts the pattern was as follows: first line manager, then higher management before regulator (22%). Similar patterns emerge where the whistleblowing process ends with an external agency other than the regulator (media or NGO). Either line manager, higher management, or both have been recipients of a speak-up concern before the whistle is blown outside. A substantial amount (12.2%) of whistleblower cases end in whistleblowers opting for a grievance route, meaning they raise their concern through a formal grievance procedure in response to the retaliation they suffer. These also tend to be protracted: half of them (50%) do so after one attempt to raise their concern elsewhere, and 26.4% after two attempts. Salient sequences involve higher management (45.3% of two attempt sequences), line managers (35.8% of two attempt sequences), or both (line manager–higher management–grievance is 28.6% of three attempt sequences). Patterns involving other recipients are specialist channel—grievance (7.5%) and line manager–external recipient–grievance (17.9%).

WHAT EXPECTATIONS DO SPEAK-UPS ENTAIL?

When people raise a concern, they communicate to someone else that they believe something in their organization is going wrong, and they expect that someone to take action. No matter what the recipient of a speak-up does after someone has raised a concern, through their response, the organization communicates something back to the whistleblower. This is the interactional view on communication, developed by Paul Watzlawick based on Gregory Bateson's 'double bind' theory. Watzlawick's theory is commonly summarized in five axioms,[25] two of which we deem crucial here to understand whistleblowing and why the source of organizational risk from whistleblowing lies in the way of responding to the whistleblower.

The first of Watzlawick's axioms that we deem crucial states that every communication consists of a content and a relationship aspect. When a worker is saying something is going wrong in the organization, they are informing someone about the wrongdoing. That is the content aspect of their communication: some facts and their evaluation of these facts as wrongdoing. There is also a relationship aspect of that communication—namely, they are also communicating that they are not able to prevent or stop that wrongdoing. They do not have to put that in actual words to communicate it. They are raising their concern precisely because they do not have the power to take action, and they assume the recipient has that power.

Watzlawick further specifies that the relationship aspect allows for interpretation of the content. Hence it is a communication about the communication, or a meta-communication. Since the relationship aspect of whistleblowing is a communication from someone who does not have power to someone who has power (or is assumed to have power), the meta-communication comes down to 'you do something about this wrongdoing'.

The second axiom of Watzlawick's communication theory we mention here is that 'one cannot *not* communicate'. If you think of behaviour, it is easy to understand that one cannot *not* behave. Even sitting still is behaviour, as is holding your breath. Because of the relationship aspect, communication is a form of behaviour. Hence, not saying anything is also a form of communication. The relationship aspect—who you are not saying anything to—will allow the other to interpret the silence. Thus 'no content' becomes content; not saying anything becomes saying nothing, and that means something.

How is this relevant to whistleblowing? So far we have established that what whistleblowers communicate is 'you must do something about this.' Because communication is interactive, once their concerns have been raised with recipients, the recipients cannot *not* communicate something back. Thus, anything the recipients do or do not do is a response. One cannot *not* respond to a whistleblower.

There are three generic ways to respond to whistleblowers: ignore, retaliate against them or take action to stop the wrongdoing. There are various ways in which whistleblowers are retaliated against (see Chapter 2), and also many kinds of action organizations could take to stop the wrongdoing, but let us keep things simple for the moment. The PCAW research[26] mentioned earlier found that when people started to speak up, 63% were ignored, 35% experienced reprisal (3% received threats and 32% experienced actual reprisal), and only 2% said they felt supported by management. The study also includes data on what people said had happened to the wrongdoing after they raised their concern: 74% felt that nothing was being done to address the wrongdoing, and only 6% indicated the wrongdoing had stopped. The other 20% said the wrongdoing was being investigated, but only half of these had confidence in the investigation.

What do these responses communicate to whistleblowers? Those who raise concerns and who get ignored may interpret the silence as an indication they are completely irrelevant, both to what goes on in the organization and as people. It is a denial of any expertise the whistleblowers might have.[27] This is different when someone raises a concern and is retaliated against. Retaliation does not communicate irrelevance. Rather, the interpretation of retaliation or the threat of retaliation makes the person raising the concern suddenly become highly relevant to what goes on in the organization. What is being communicated in this scenario is that he or she is a threat to the status quo, that is, maintaining the wrongdoing.[28] Research shows that retaliation against those who raise concerns inside their organizations makes it more likely that those people will go on and raise their concerns outside the organization.[29] The response that they are relevant but annoying acknowledges that the person is 'on to something': that their concerns are not misguided. In that sense, retaliation can trigger the self-identification of someone with a concern as a whistleblower. It can also make it very clear to the person raising the concern what the terms of the game are—namely, that they are expected to keep quiet.

Frederick Bird[30] wrote about the phenomenon of organizations where people get signals that voicing of concerns is not wanted. He calls this phenomenon the 'muted conscience', and distinguishes between moral muteness on the one hand and hypocrisy on the other. Whereas hypocrites voice moral concerns they do not possess, moral muteness occurs when people fail to voice the moral concerns they do hold and therefore also often fail to act upon them. Moral muteness is enforced by expressions of moral deafness (i.e. ignoring those who raise concerns) and moral blindness (for example, refusing to see the concerns when they are raised and instead seeing the people raising it as annoyance).

Among the factors creating a muted conscience are lack of accountability, organizational barriers to dissent, fear of involvement, weak conscience, and a sense of futility. Using Bird's terminology then, it can be said then that responding to people who raise concerns by ignoring them or by retaliating against them enforces a muted conscience. Ignoring them makes the voicing of a moral concern futile and weakens their conscience. Retaliating against them creates a fear of involvement, acknowledges a lack of accountability, and creates a barrier to any dissent.

The point is that any response to someone raising a concern not only communicates something back to the person raising the concern, but in itself is a communication about the moral consciousness that is present in the organization to the wrongdoer, other managers, and future potential whistleblowers. Hence, in responding to whistleblowers there is a feedback loop that goes not only to the whistleblower but to everyone in the organization, as depicted in Figure 4.2.

Ignoring whistleblowers communicates to them that they are irrelevant to what goes on in the organization. To wrongdoers it communicates that there is a lack of accountability in the organization and hence that their wrongdoing will not hamper the success of the organization. It communicates to future potential

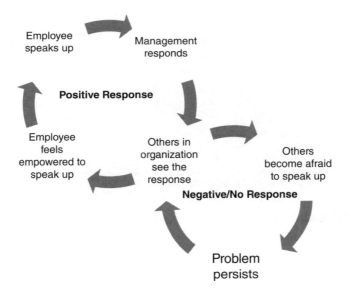

FIGURE 4.2 Organizational feedback loop when responding to a whistleblower

whistleblowers that raising a concern is futile, and denies them any involvement in achieving organizational outcomes beyond what they are told to do. In short, it kills engagement and tells people not to care about the organization they work in. This is a dangerous situation because it is the perfect recipe for small wrongdoings to grow into disasters.

Retaliating against whistleblowers will have similar effects but might speed things up. It communicates to wrongdoers that the organization is on their side, and might indicate to the wrongdoers and others that the wrongdoing is beneficial to the organization. Corrupt business models might work in short term, but in the long term they either fail or waste a lot of resources and time when trying to get things back on track. To future potential whistleblowers retaliation induces a fear of involvement and leaves them with three choices: to join in on the wrongdoing, leave the organization, or blow the whistle outside the organization. As noted earlier, retaliation communicates to the whistleblower that he or she is on to something. If this triggers them to self-identify as whistleblowers, it becomes more likely that they will blow the whistle outside of the organization to a regulator or to the media. Hence, retaliating against internal whistleblowers allows small wrongdoings to grow into disasters more quickly, and also makes it more likely that external actors will intervene. If that happens, whatever the wrongdoing was, it has become a disaster for the organization.

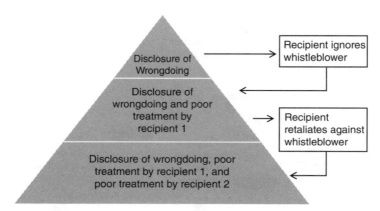

FIGURE 4.3 Information about wrongdoing and about responses in whistleblowing

The wrongdoing that occurs when concerns are ignored or employees who speak up are retaliated against, is another type of wrongdoing by the organization. It is wrongdoing because it denies the person their moral consciousness, their sense of expertise, and their engagement. It is also wrongdoing because it will allow the reported behaviour to go on or even become more severe. This behaviour by the organization is then enforced through the feedback loop that communicates not only to the whistleblower but to everyone in the organization that the concern is not valid or the wrong behaviour is acceptable.

A second implication emerges when we take into regard Watzlawick's theory of communication, and the meta-communications or the relationship aspect of responding to whistleblowers by retaliating against them or ignoring them. If silence tells them they are irrelevant and denies them their expertise, and if reprisal tells them they are annoying, what happens when they try to raise their concern again? Their concern will include both facts about the wrongdoing and emotions and facts about how they have been responded to previously. As Figure 4.3 depicts, the implication is that the story a whistleblower tells becomes more muddied with every attempt he or she makes. This not only makes it harder for the recipient to focus on the initial wrongdoing, but the treatment of the whistleblower is now a second wrongdoing that needs to be addressed as well. Research in the Netherlands[31] on confidential advisors in organizations confirms this. In this study researchers found that the main task of the speak-up advisors was to unravel facts from emotions and coach the advisee in raising their concern in an effective, factual way.

So far we have discussed ignoring and retaliating against whistleblowers. What about the third generic response—namely, taking action to stop the wrongdoing? This can mean different things: investigating the concern or the allegations, passing information on to someone who is mandated, resourced, and competent to do these investigations, intervening to change practices and behaviour of staff, and sanctioning the wrongdoer.

It is tempting to think of whistleblowing in isolation from the organizational context in which it always occurs. The idea then amounts to a straightforward plan: take the concern seriously, investigate the alleged wrongdoing, correct the wrongdoing, and sanction the wrongdoer. When people argue for better whistleblower protection, or for improved whistleblowing policies in general, this is also how they envision the journey: as a procedure that runs unpunctured and undisrupted from the moment the concern is raised to when the wrongdoing is stopped. As we saw in the last chapter, however, this is not the case. Concerns are raised in different ways, to different people at different times. A perfect process could only happen if the world would stop the moment the concern is raised and would start moving again once the investigation of the wrongdoing has taken place and the sanctions have been decided. Unfortunately this assumption simply does not hold. The world keeps turning, and the organization keeps moving, as does everyone in it.

Anechiarico and Jacobs[32] argue that as an instrument to detect wrongdoing, speak-up arrangements also bring an efficiency cost to organizations. Writing in the context of government administration, they note how investigations following a speak-up can paralyse a whole department, as the agency head refuses to act out of fear of triggering criticism while investigations are under way. They cite a case where the investigations took six years to complete.[33] Organizations cannot afford such paralysis, but while they need to continue to function well and smoothly, there needs to be trust that wrongdoing will nevertheless be stopped. That is a huge challenge. What happens when a concern is raised is a 'disorganization'.[34] The management problem becomes a people problem. How to correct the wrongdoing remains neatly within a standard management process of planning, delegating, monitoring, and correcting. For the people problem however—how to maintain, restore and reconfigure cooperation between people—there are no simple heuristics. To develop an answer we must look to the complexities of trust in organizations. In the next section we present insights on how trust relationships evolve throughout the whistleblowing process from the point of view of the speak-up operator—the recipient of internal whistleblowing.

CHALLENGES OF OPERATING SPEAK-UP ARRANGEMENTS

A practice of speaking up that is both safe and effective relies on organizational cultures that are conducive to open discussion of concerns. We write this book from the position that such cultures can and need to be nurtured, and that effective speak-up arrangements are crucial in doing so. Too often organizations mistakenly assume that declaring an 'open door' policy creates an 'open door' culture. Yet cultures are not created by mere declaration. Carlos[35] studied the effectiveness of a range of voice channels and found that informal 'open door' policies either work well or fail miserably. Hence relying on informal 'open door' policies is too risky, especially in complex organizations. As introduced in Chapter 2, whistleblowing research notes the importance of trust for internal whistleblowing that is both effective and safe.[36] When trust exists, employees are more likely to speak up, and also more likely to do so internally rather than externally.[37] Conversely, if there is a culture of silence, as was described in some of the sectors in Chapter 3, or when there is little organizational support for speaking up, individuals may find it wiser to keep quiet.[38] However, trust has so far not been a central concept in whistleblowing research. Perhaps this is because whistleblowing has mainly been studied as a one-off event rather than a process in the context of whistleblowing,[39] and, as discussed in Chapter 2, the idea that trust is largely seen as a static part of organization culture. The literature on trust however, has theorized it as a process in which time is a key dimension for examining how it happens and evolves, through interactions between truster and trustee.[40] Further on in this chapter, we will draw explicitly on theories of trust as a process to explore how speak-up operators attempt to make the speak-up arrangement trustworthy.

Three of the organizations in Chapter 3 had introduced their speak-up arrangement in response to a crisis of trust. In one of our case organizations, this crisis was triggered by wrongdoing involving the organization, which led to police raiding their offices, and to substantial regulatory sanctions. In another organization, regulators carried out inspections following a whistleblower concern being raised with them. In a third case organization, the crisis in trust was triggered by scandals in the industry, rather than wrongdoing involving the company itself. None of these organizations had time to rebuild trust before implementing a speak-up arrangement. Instead, they rebuilt trust *through* the implementation of their speak-up arrangement. In our research we noticed how the speak-up arrangements in the organizations *shaped* practices of trust, rather than *relying on* trust. Hence, trust appears as a continuous process involving: practices that change over time, the supported independence of speak-up operators, and in some cases outsider trust.

Time

Our research shows how speak-up arrangements change the way people practice trust in organizations over time (see Box 4.2). The three organizations differ with regard to how long they have been trying to implement speak-up arrangements. During interviews, many individuals shared reflections on the evolution of the arrangements and interactions they and others have had with the new systems. For example, in one of the organizations the speak-up arrangement was implemented as part of an organizational overhaul of the compliance function. This function was centralized to give it more independence from operational matters, and the number of compliance officers grew tenfold. The organization has had multiple speak-up channels in place for almost a decade now. Initially a channel through which employees could ask integrity-related questions, rather than report alleged wrongdoing, was used the most. Subsequently the organization saw more employees raising concerns through the externally operated hotline. More recently, in most of the regions where the company operates, the way employees voice concerns has shifted to open and direct communication. Hence, there appears to be a shift in the channel that is preferred by employees: from an initial preference for asking integrity-related questions through a web interface, over time to directly raising concerns. It is possible that familiarity and positive experiences with one channel transfers trust to other channels, and that past experiences of trust enable future experiences.[41] It also indicates that the resourcing for, and organizational position of, the compliance function can support the process of trusting within the organization with regard to voicing concerns.

BOX 4.2   KENNY ON TIME AND WHISTLEBLOWING]

Kenny[42] *researched notions of time in relation to whistleblowing, showing perceptions of time can act as an obstacle to effective resistance but also that long-term interpretations of time can alleviate anxieties around whistleblowing experiences, focusing on financial services organizations. Kenny's study focuses on time from a whistleblower's point of view, for example, how whistleblowers' self-perceptions change throughout successive unsuccessful whistleblowing to various recipients. We know that people try to speak-up a concern more than once,*[43] *most often first with the wrongdoer directly or with their line manager. When this is not successful, they then tend to either turn to someone else within the organization or seek an external recipient (regulator or media). It often takes a number of attempts to raise a concern before the disclosed information is investigated. This investigation also takes time.*

Changes in practices of trust do not only involve employees. We also noted an evolution in how management is practicing trust through speak-up arrangements. One organization had recently moved the oversight of the speak-up arrangement from the compliance function to the HR function at group level. This was done to support a change of 'tone' with regard to speaking up, widening the scope of concerns taken into account and emphasising well-being and engagement rather than 'policing'. At the same time, the organization started to promote an additional channel through which employees could get free and independent advice on how to raise concerns and how the law protects them.

These changes to the *how* of trusting—rather than simply altering levels of trust—correspond with changes in professional identity of those operating speak-up arrangements. Compliance officers from our case organizations noted that the speak-up arrangement had played a role in changing how employees perceived them. Where they used to be considered 'police' they felt they were now perceived more as 'someone who can help'. An HR officer said she saw it as a compliment when employees trusted her enough to raise concerns with her.

Independence

A crucial characteristic of effective speak-up arrangements appears to be the level of independence of the speak-up operator. The secondary interview data we used showed that a lack of independence of the speak-up operators leads to ineffective whistleblowing and a general distrust towards top management. This resonates with our primary interview data with speak-up operators from the three organizations, in the sense that their level of independence from day-to-day operational matters also gives them trust in their professionalism.

> *We only go upwards to group audit committee. There's no coming down or anywhere. We haven't got accountability to anywhere else in the business. (Bank interviewee N)*
>
> *But if I look at one of the advantages that we have with my role—I'm not a business partner. So if you were running this through the HR business partners, they're a little bit too close [to top management]. Whereas I'm not aligned to any one of the individual business team, so that gives me the added opportunity to be more independent.' (Bank interviewee K)*

For the speak-up operators, the perception of independence was based on their specialist role and rule-bound referrals. We use the term 'rule-bound referrals' for protocols and policies that specify rules for managers at different levels about how, when, and to whom within the organization concerns raised by employees must be escalated.

Specialist Speak-up Operators   Where receiving and following-up speak-up concerns was their core task rather than a marginal aspect of their job description, speak-up operators were able to keep focus on appropriate listening, provide objective evaluation of the quality of investigations, and oversee and document end-to-end follow-up of concerns. They were also able to spot potential wrongdoing underlying concerns that at first seemed unsubstantial or unfounded.

Interviewees gave us examples of concerns that would have been ignored before the speak-up arrangement was in place, but were now looked into. There were also examples where the compliance function had initially referred a concern to the specialist HR speak-up operator because they believed it had no compliance-related content. When the HR officer looked into the matter however, issues were uncovered that had relevance for compliance but were not initially mentioned by the employee.

In all organizations, at least half of the concerns raised through speak-up channels were not about wrongdoing in the sense of harm to the public interest, breach of regulation, or breach of organizational policy. Specialist speak-up operators tend not to disregard such concerns as an 'employee grievance' or as just a nuisance. Instead, they are able to perceive what seem at first to be people-related concerns, as potential signals of underlying risks relating to operations, people management or compliance. This is supported by research carried out into best practice for speak up systems by Australian public sector organizations, which notes that a successful approach is to integrate all types of reported wrongdoing including personal, employment and workplace grievances.[44] This is because these are often complex and intertwined with genuine whistleblowing concerns.

Rule-bound Referrals How speak-up operators perceived their independence was influenced by organizational policies that included rule-bound referrals of employee speak-up concerns. These restrict the discretion of both managers as well as speak-up operators with regard to referring employee concerns for investigation. Speak-up operators felt these rules supported them in investigating concerns that could lead to sanctions against managers. They also gave examples where these rule-bound referrals mandated them to take action in case local managers wanted to 'wait and see' how things developed, or wanted to handle the concern themselves. The organizations had worked out flow-charts for rule-bound referrals.

> *If I look into the cases that arise in the organization, whenever I have a case and it looks a little bit like corruption, the HR colleagues do not like it if I give them to the compliance organization. So they say 'we should deal with it on our own, and it's not such a difficult case, and it's not so serious' and so on. [...] It's easy for me because my managers give me backing [...] and I can say 'if we don't give it to them, and the case escalates, then we are part of the problem. Please be part of the solution and not part of the problem.' (Engineering company interviewee C)*

Independence of speak-up operators is a crucial characteristic of effective speak-up arrangements. Our research shows that this independence must be reflected in the design of, and support for, speak-up arrangements. Overall implementing speak-up arrangements that include specialist speak-up operator roles and rule-bound referrals helped in making the organizational speak-up process trustworthy.

Outsider Independence As mentioned in Chapter 2, external independent advice operators are fundamentally distinct from externally operated hotlines or external ombudspersons. External independent advice operators maintain a legal privilege with the voicing employee. They offer advice in the interest of the whistleblower. When internal voice is ineffective or leads to retaliation, these external advisers will guide voicing employees to the appropriate regulator, as well as inform them about their rights and available avenues under the whistleblower protection legislation. Two of the three organizations in our research promoted an external advice line as part of their speak-up arrangement.

> *When I first took over this job I thought they were a place where people could actually report. But their service is not that. They never take reports from individuals and escalate them to us. What they position themselves as is an advisory line. So if I think there is something wrong and I ring them and I say, 'I think this kind of thing has happened and what do I do and how do I go about it and whatever?' Their role there is talk me through the process to talk to me about the potential impacts on me, what I might have to go through in terms of investigation, et cetera, et cetera. And then to leave me to make a decision with regard to whether I will proceed with that or not. And therefore, all we get from them is numbers. [...] Very high added value for us. [...] that's most useful because—particularly, we would talk to our colleague financial services companies and we're worried at the very low numbers of speak-up calls—there'd be less than one a month [...] And on the one hand you say, 'Well, that's a good thing.' On the other hand you'd say, 'Well, does that mean that it's not trusted?' And so the debate goes on all the time in terms of, well, we would maintain that nothing significantly untoward that should have been found out by a speak-up—should not have happened and wasn't raised by a speak-up. We haven't seen anything like that and that is one of the things we check. (Bank interviewee H)*

Contrary to what one might expect, speak-up operators from these organizations did not see the presence of an independent advice line for employees as a threat to their role. In fact, they perceived that facilitating employees to seek their own advice, made the speak-up arrangement more trustworthy, even when that opportunity was hardly ever used.

Responsiveness

In the research literature, informal voice is defined as ideas or concerns expressed directly and outside of a structured process.[45] Formal voice is where the idea or concern is registered according to specific processes, and a systematic evaluation of the voiced idea or concern is made. In the organizations we researched speak-up arrangements always implied a formalization of voice in two ways: voice is increasingly registered, and response to voice is increasingly prescribed for managers at all levels.

TABLE 4.4   Centralisation of speak-up data in the three organizations

	Director of Corporate Affairs	Head of Strategic HR	Central Compliance
Hospital	X		
Bank		X	
Engineering Company			X

Registering Speak-up Events   The additional provision of voice channels, that is, internal key persons, question channels, and internal or external hotlines provide opportunities for a centralised documenting of voice. Table 4.4 gives an overview of where voice data is centralised in the three organizations. It must be noted however that the organizations differed with regard to the extent to which they registered speak-up voice. Some of the organizations were still deliberating on what exactly to register as a 'speak-up'. The engineering company had the most developed policy on registering voice. This was also the organization with the longest track history of operating the speak-up arrangement.

In the hospital, concerns formally raised under the speak-up policy are registered as speak-up events. This means that voiced concerns to local managers would not be registered, but concerns voiced verbally or written with internal key persons would. Anything voiced—concerns and questions— through the internal hotline is also recorded. The Director of Corporate Affairs maintains the register and reports every six months to the Audit Committee. The external independent advice line does not allow management to record the individual concerns raised with them. It is possible that an employee will voice a concern with a key internal person or through the internal hotline after seeking independent advice. The independent advice operator only provides management with aggregated numbers of concerns.

The bank requires its internal key persons to advise voicing employees on whether their concern would best be treated as a grievance or as a speak-up. They are required to formally register speak-up voice after which the Head of Strategic HR takes over as contact for the voicing employee and coordinator of the investigation. An employee writing a letter to the CEO to voice a concern however, would not necessarily or automatically be registered or treated as a speak-up. It appeared from our interviews at the bank that a policy on what to record as a speak-up had not fully crystallised yet. The ownership of the speak-up arrangement had recently changed hands from compliance to HR, and the bank was in the process of deciding who would be their 'speak-up champion' in response to the FCA regulator requirement. Some were thinking about a more integrated formalisation of voice:

> *the broad definition of speak-up is somebody picking up a phone, or send-ing an email through a designated line or email address [...] We'd have it through other formats but it's not actually categorised as speak-up, if that makes sense. So we're actually missing a trick in classification. (Bank interviewee N)*

The engineering company went furthest in registering voice. Not only were concerns voiced through the question channel logged, but also local compliance and local HR managers were required to record concerns containing a compli-ance aspect. Central compliance monitors patterns emerging from the integrated database. The company produces manuals for managers at all levels on how and when to record voice. For interviewees at this organization, this formalisation of voice at the recording stage was one of the key changes in responding to voice. Before the overhaul of their speak-up arrangement, they did not register anony-mous reports.

Liaising functions and division of labour   We found that the responsiveness of orga-nizations is further enabled when speak-up arrangements are not operated from one single function. Coordination between different functions such as compliance and HR, liaised with each other through clear protocols allows a division of labour in which each function applies its specialism.

At the bank, it is strategic HR who owns the speak-up arrangement and liaises with the special investigations unit (SIU). HR's function is to 'mantle' the voicing employee and follow up their well-being, whilst SIU investigates the potential wrongdoing.

> *And when a report comes in, that's always the first point of contact we would make. And they're effectively the internal professional investiga-tors. So there's that and there's also—we have a very strong protocol around protecting the individual by checking their comfort levels, they're—supporting them. So keeping a very distinct split between the case manager, who typically will probably be someone in HR—someone like me or [...]—and the investigator. Having very, very clear divisions of responsibility. (Bank interviewee K)*

In the engineering company, central compliance owned the speak-up arrangement. However, this does not mean compliance deals with everything. Much of the concerns voiced through the speak-up channels are HR related issues rather than compliance issues. The engineering company has a designated HR officer at headquarters to whom compliance refers the HR related concerns, and who investigates, sometimes devolving these and following up with regional levels. It also occurs that what appears to be an HR related matter turns out to have a compliance element to it. Hence, although compliance owns the speak-up arrangement, it liaises with the HR function under a clear protocol.

Making Responding the Norm   The organizations in our research were also increasingly being prescriptive with regard to responding to voice. However, this might not necessarily be a general trend. Some interviewees told us they still knew many organizations where management was focusing on encouraging people to speak-up rather than paying attention to how concerns are responded to.

> *How did we have it before the scandal? We did not have an organization like compliance, and whoever had the case on the desk decided how to deal with it. Because of that we had a lot of cases that went into the basket, but they were worth investigating, otherwise we would not have this scandal. (Engineering company interviewee D)*

A lack of responsiveness is mainly an outcome of managers' fear of negative feedback and implicit beliefs often held by managers, that is, 'management knows best' and 'unity is good and dissent is bad'.[46] Managers receiving voice can feel threatened and might want to avoid embarrassment or feelings of incompetence and vulnerability. In our research we found that those operating speak-up arrangements seem to be aware of these managerial tendencies and make attempts to tackle them. In other words merely formalising voice channels is not enough; they need to be embedded in such a way that managerial tendencies to deny or neglect concerns are subverted. One way this was done at the bank was by reinforcing the message that responding to voice is part of a managers' job and retaliating is both a disciplinary as well as a legal breach.

> *I'm not saying all managers are bad eggs out there but I'm saying that they need to be driving this themselves, and not just be left to a HR function to issue policies and procedures every so often, once a year. [...] That needs to be on the forefront of people's minds that this is an avenue to go down. (Bank interviewee N)*
>
> *But there's no doubt about it: you have to do it as part of the overall agenda where we're saying to line managers, 'It is your responsibility to listen.' And sometimes line managers keep saying, 'Well, I have my own job to do,' and we have to keep saying, 'No, you're the people manager*

and part of your responsibility is to listen and to act and to respond'.
(Bank interviewee H)

The continuous reinforcement of this message is important. A model of manager responsiveness based on the theory of planned behaviour posits that the way
managers will respond to employee concerns is influenced by the manager's personal beliefs about whistleblowing, social norm cues the manager receives about
responding, and the manager's perceived behavioural control for responding.[47]
The term 'perceived behaviour control' refers to someone's perception of the ease
or difficulty of performing a specific behaviour. Thus, managers might personally believe it is good that employees voice concerns, and they might also receive
cues from higher management that it is important to respond to these concerns,
but if managers do not know how to respond or do not feel adequately mandated
to respond, they might still neglect the concern.

The rule-bound referrals mentioned earlier can influence managers' perceived
behavioural control. But speak-up operators seemed to be an important way of
signalling the norm throughout the organization about responding to employee
concerns.

BARRIERS TO RESPONSIVENESS

The literature on employee voice suggests that from an employee perspective one
of the key attributes of effective voice systems is credibility, and that employees
perceive managers as fair when they provide accounts and explanations for decisions.[48] Our research with speak-up operators finds that in the context of concerns
about wrongdoing, giving account and explanation is not always straightforward.
There are three main reasons for this: anonymous concerns, legal limitations, and
the invisibility of response.

Anonymous Concerns

Communicating back to people who voiced their concerns anonymously is difficult, if not impossible. Even when from a manager's point of view the organization
is responding to the concern, it is not possible to also have it perceived as such from
the employees' point of view. Employees who speaks up might be mistaken about
their concern, in which case they will not see any management intervention into a
practice they mistakenly perceive as wrongdoing.

I do have one that ran last year where an individual invoked the right to
raise it on an anonymous basis. They sent it in in paper format. We inves-
tigated it. They have sent that speak-up in three times now, but because
they've remained anonymous, we can't go back to them to tell them we've

looked at it seriously, we've investigated it, we haven't been able to back up the claims, we don't have any more additional information. (Bank interviewee H)

Before the hospital reviewed their speak-up arrangement, an anonymous concern had been escalated to board level, but the investigation had not been quick enough to prevent the employee from perceiving the concern as being ignored. The employee blew the whistle to the regulator, who authorised an inspection.

Anonymous speak-up often occurs through a purposely made email account, for example, whistle333@hotmail.com. Whilst the speak-up operator would be able to communicate further with the employee through that account, the problem is that employees often create such an account to raise the concern but then fail to check it after that, making it a *de facto* one-way anonymous communication. This can also create an additional barrier to responsiveness because it is not possible to ask for additional information about the alleged wrongdoing.

Legal Issues

Speak-up operators in addition to other interviewees told us that communicating the outcome of an investigation is necessarily limited on legal grounds. Conveying details can inhibit legal proceedings against a wrongdoer. But privacy and data protection regulation also limit what can be communicated about an investigation or outcome. This regulation differs between countries (see Box 4.3). Hence, communications about investigations and outcomes are nearly always vague. This may create the impression with the voicing employee that their concern is not taken seriously.

BOX 4.3   PRIVACY AND DATA PROTECTION REGULATION: SOME DIFFERENCES BETWEEN COUNTRIES

In Europe, the General Data Protection Regulation took effect on May 25, 2018. The EU General Data Protection Regulation (GDPR) replaces the Data Protection Directive 95/46/EC and was 'designed to harmonize data privacy laws across Europe, to protect and empower all EU citizens data privacy and to reshape the way organizations across the region approach data privacy' (https://www.eugdpr.org/). The new legislation has several key changes including expanded scope—it applies to all companies processing the personal data of data subjects residing in the Union, regardless of the company's location; stiffer penalties for breaches—4% of the organization's

(Continued)

global annual turnover or 20 million euros, whichever is more—and tougher rules around gaining consent, including the need to present the terms of use in layman's terms instead of lengthy legal jargon.

The United States has a much less cohesive approach to the issue and relies on some sector-specific national laws and hundreds of state-specific laws designed for various sectors, uses, and audiences. California alone has more than 25 state laws on data protection and privacy. This complex legal environment and accompanying loopholes has recently led to massive amounts of personal data being used by companies like Cambridge Analytica for ethically questionable causes. While the legality of such data mining is being investigated by congress at the time of writing, the legal landscape remains difficult to understand and navigate for the general population.[49]

Invisibility of the Response

Even when sanctions are taken against a wrongdoer, these are not always visible. For example, a minor wrongdoing might be sanctioned by a reprimand or a formal warning. Nevertheless, it is the perceived response rather than the real response that matters for individual and collective sense making about how responsive management is, and hence how effective or futile raising a concern is.

STRATEGIES FOR TRUSTWORTHINESS (AND THEIR POTENTIAL PITFALLS)

Because whistleblowing is a protracted process, studying notions of trust in the progression of disclosures requires using a process view of trust, in which interactions over time play an important role. Central to the notion of 'trust as process' or 'trusting' is the temporal nature of trust. In Chapter 2, we introduced trust as continuous and dynamic rather than momentary and static.[50] Nooteboom[51] critiques transaction costs economics (TCE) by arguing that although TCE acknowledges the importance of time lapses, parameters of trust are nevertheless assumed as unchanging. Yet, if we research ongoing interactions, it is unreasonable to ignore that perceptions about past interactions, propensities towards opportunism, and possibilities of building trust are formed during these repeated interactions. Adobor[52] and Jagd[53] argue in a similar direction—namely, that earlier experiences can provide small cues that, through a process of sense making, are subsequently enlarged through accumulation of evidence, which may lead to behavioural changes instantiating alternative or additional forms of trust. Hence how trusting in organizations changes and evolves is essential when studying trust as a process. Following Möllering,[54] we provide in this section insights into how speak-up operators attempt to support trust between whistleblower, speak-up operator, and the organization (see Box 4.4).

BOX 4.4   TRUST AS EXPECTATION

Trust is a complex social phenomenon that appears in many forms, depending on the context and the type and stage of exchange relationship involved[55] *and has also been theorized—often in contrasting ways—according to the disciplinary traditions within which it has been examined.*[56] *If we put a general definition of trust next to that of whistleblowing, we see that both phenomena revolve around expectation. Trust is:*

A state of favourable expectation regarding other people's actions and intentions.[57]

Möllering[58] *further develops the notion of 'trust as expectation' by revisiting Simmel's thinking on trust. Accordingly, trust is a mental process that encompasses the elements of expectation, interpretation and suspension. More precisely, trust as 'a state of favourable expectation' is an outcome of a dynamic combination of cognitive interpretations of lived experience and noncognitive suspensions which amount to a bracketing or indifference towards what remains uncertain or unknown. McEvily*[59] *arrives at a similar hybrid conceptualisation of trust, as a combination of probabilistic and heuristic decision-making. Probabilistic decision-making involves a conscious calculation of risk, whereas heuristic decision-making involves intuitive and automatic judgments. Both McEvily and Möllering*[60] *assert that if risk were fully calculable there would be no need for trust. In that sense 'trust is characterized by insufficient information and emotionally enabled leaps of faith'.*[61]

Adjacent to the process view of 'trust as continuing' is the process view of 'trust as becoming'.[62] If trust needs to be continuously (re)produced, and positive trust experiences enhance the truster's well-being, professional identities are central to the process of trusting. Repeated negative trusting experiences adversely impact the mental health of employees who speak up.[63] Our research provides insights into how experiences around speak-up can be seen as changing the *how* of trusting rather than simply altering levels of trust, and how this corresponds with changes in professional identity. Möllering[64] emphasizes that trusting is not only formative for individual identity but also for collective identity: 'trusting signals and confirms an actor's willingness to belong to a collective'.[65] It is crucial to include this in a study of practices of trusting that emerge around the implementation of speak-up arrangements in organizations because such management interventions are often linked to stated values and rules of the organization in codes of conduct.[66] Möllering's sketch (2013) of the process view on 'trusting as constituting' suggests however that trusting is not simply dependent on the organizational context, that is, the trusting that emerges around speak-up arrangements is not determined by the conjoining-values statement. Trusting as constituting implies that rules and resources in which speak-up arrangements are embedded (such as organizational values) are (re)produced.

Our interviewees were of the view that employees normally raise a concern about wrongdoing with their line manager, and only use a speak-up channel when there is a lack of trust between the employee and this person. This was always perceived as a lack of intentional trust; the employee believes the line manager does not want to look into the concern. Our interviewees phrased this in terms of employees fearing that the manager would retaliate. In addition, speak-up operators themselves perceived employees to often lack trust in them. They phrased this in terms of lack of competence trust; the employee believes the designated speak-up recipient lacks the ability to look into the concern. For example, our multinational organization uses an external ombudsperson based in central Europe. Our interviewees were convinced employees from Latin America did not use the ombudsperson to speak up because they believed the ombudsperson would not be able to understand their language. Another example is where interviewees found it hard to explain to employees what the process was that the compliance office used to maintain the whistleblower's identity confidential. This resulted in the employees' lack of trust in the compliance officer's competence to maintain confidentiality. These are instances where people lack 'good reasons', and are not able to make the 'leap of faith'.[67]

Our interviewees acknowledged that if they were not successful in being trustworthy, employees would blow the whistle externally. Hence, speak-up operators made various interventions in an attempt to allow employees to trust internal speak-up channels. If the organization fails to convey an expectation to the whistleblower that he or she will be taken seriously and treated well—for instance by providing and sharing the case of successful whistleblowing—this could lead to the whistleblower turning to an external recipient such as a regulator or media resulting in the scandal causing additional costs to the organization. Hence speak-up operators have an incentive to behave well towards whistleblowers.

Creating Trust

Organizations task speak-up operators with being trustworthy recipients so that the whistleblowing can remain inside the organization. Our interviewees understood this task in a number of ways. Some had been able to adjust the speak-up arrangement by empathizing with the whistleblower:

> *What did we have beforehand, you have to access the policy via the Internet, you've got to read through it, it's quite complicated. You think, 'Do I*

really want to do this?' You're putting yourself out there as well, because it's not necessarily anonymous.

Apart from simplifying the procedure, some speak-up operators mentioned the importance of the interaction interface. In one organization they would arrange to meet secretly with a whistleblower so as not to scare them away from further interactions should they require more information from the whistleblower. In another organization a pilot using an automated voice intake on the hotline was abandoned in favour of a real person on the other side of the line. They believed a human interface was more effective in getting the necessary information from a whistleblower to carry out an investigation. A US-based compliance officer from our Engineering company added that:

Call-in systems with human interface was traditionally what was used in the United States and we just had a sense that it would just make Americans—North Americans and maybe others in other countries— a bit more comfortable to talk to a person about these issues.

Making the interaction 'more comfortable' and more aligned with 'tradition' can be seen as attempts to make the 'leap of faith' or suspension easier, so that it becomes easier for the whistleblower to have trust. Interviewees from the multinational organization had noticed that the speak-up channel peaked after someone from the central compliance office had made a country visit to explain the speak-up arrangements to staff.

Other strategies to become trustworthy were enacted at the time the speak-up operater first met with a whistleblower. What some operators did was to emphasize the independence of the compliance office ('their eyes light up ... we're going to listen impartially'), or telling the whistleblower that they are being interviewed as a witness so that they are not a discloser but more another person in the story.

Speak-up operators tend to evaluate their trustworthiness in terms of the number of times speak-up channels were used. In one organization, which had been running its speak-up arrangement for almost 10 years, interviewees understood the success of their attempts to build trust as a combination of lower usage of the hotline or web-based interface, and an increased proportion of whistleblowers approaching compliance officers directly via email or in person. They explained this as an outcome of them being perceived differently by employees:

In the beginning we were mostly considered as police. More and more they see you as a trusted advisor, because of frequent interactions.

In other organizations, interviewees were not sure how to interpret low numbers of people whistleblowing through the speak-up channels. Did it mean people did not feel the necessity to use them—for instance, did this mean they trusted the wrongdoer or the line manager to take action—or did it mean that people did not trust the speak-up operators? In one organization speak-up operators suspected that not everything that should be raised through a speak-up channel actually was, and that currently people were phrasing their concern about wrongdoing as grievances:

> *In this organization [...] there's enough of a hierarchy in terms of that person's leader or the head of the area. So it goes up in rank. And I think that's why we see people invoking formal grievances as opposed to going into the speak-up because they feel, 'I've had the conversation with my line manager's line manager in relation to whatever the issues is because I don't feel I can talk to my immediate line manager but I'm still not getting what I want. So I'll go through this process.'*

Note the interviewee invokes a failure on his or her part to support employees in making the noncognitive ('feel') leap of trust required for speaking up. Another organization had concluded numbers alone did not allow them to evaluate the trustworthiness of their speak-up channels and had turned to a third party to benchmark and certify them.

Hence we found that whistleblowing occurs in a context of lack of trust. The whistleblower has no trust that the wrongdoer or the line manager will stop the wrongdoing or refrain from retaliation. Speak-up operators seemed to believe they needed to create trust between themselves and the whistleblowers in order to avoid external whistleblowing. In this sense potential recipients of whistleblowing (internal and external) appear to compete for the whistleblower's trust. Internal speak-up operators made interventions at both the cognitive level ('good reasons') as well as the noncognitive level ('leap of faith') for creating the expectation with the whistleblower that they would behave favorably. Though initially the number of people making use of them evidences the trust in speak-up channels, eventually the trustworthiness of the organization that has implemented the speak-up channels emerges as is evidenced by a drop in people using them, which is offset by more direct whistleblowing through personal contacts with speak-up operators.

Maintaining Trust

Accommodating whistleblowers to 'win' their trust can put that trust at risk once the concern is investigated. Our interview data contained instances where speak-up operators acknowledged it was hard for them to deliver on the signaling they undertook to get employees to blow the whistle to them.

> *If you whistle blow for something small, that's not really the thing. If you're more senior, and you whistle blow, so the people who are discussing the issue will know. If you're senior enough, if you're in the top 500 [in this organization], you'd be known. [...] I don't think it can be as anonymous as you'd like to think. It would definitely not be talked about openly, but—You know the thing about 'I told everyone to keep it a*

secret.' [. . .] if you involved the committee, and the investigation team,
compliance or whoever, the HR team. At least 15.

Hence the more the speak-up operators signal the anonymity and confidentiality of a speak-up channel, the more they put up an act involving a promise they know they cannot keep. We also found instances where the competence-based trust that whistleblowers might have makes it difficult for the speak-up operator to deliver:

[. . .] people usually imagine the compliance officer can do whatever they
want, and it is not like that.

Speak-up operators are restricted in what they can do for whistleblowers and when or whether they can start an investigation. This is because the speak-up operator is not a fiduciary to the whistleblower. Rather, the speak-up operator has to balance different trust relationships. For example, some interviewees mentioned that their role involved both protecting the whistleblower as well as protecting the organization from malicious whistleblowing. Indeed, a number of interviewees implicitly turned the question of trust around: asking what would be the basis for them to trust a whistleblower. Another example of their limitation relates to the kind of agency a speak-out operator has. An interviewee explained that an ombudsperson will be 'credible to the whistleblower' if the ombudsperson can make management listen in a way that the average employee cannot. Yet the ombudsperson will only have this agency if he or she is also 'credible to the management' in the sense that management trusts the ombudsperson is competent at filtering out the unimportant and frivolous concerns. This is an example of the behavioural trust that was introduced in Chapter 2. A third example of the restriction of speak-up operators' agency is where the concerns raised are broad professional issues rather than cases of concrete wrongdoing:

The sort of issues that get escalated are quite broad issues. An example
at the moment is one of our anesthetists feels that anesthesia isn't given
enough prominence in the hospital. And that's a really broad concept, and
in personal discussions, and in written responses to that individual, I've
both tried to address the concerns and responded. But even so, there is
still a perception on that individual's part that they've still not got special
prominence.

Möllering[68] notes that trust brings about a moral obligation. The truster's expectation that the trustee will behave in a certain way makes the trustee feel morally obliged to behave that way. The speak-up operators we interviewed seemed to feel such obligation, but it was not clear whether this was merely because whistleblowers trusted them, or partly also because they themselves had created specific expectations they could not deliver on. In this sense, a trustee's betrayal of the truster might not only find its root in behaving differently from what the truster expects, but also in the signaling that the trustee undertakes to allow the truster's interpretation and suspension leading to trust.

We found that speak-up operators also attempted to manage trust at the post-investigation stage. Our interviewees sometimes struggled with getting the whistleblower to accept the outcome of an investigation. Even that there had been a serious investigation at all, was sometimes doubted by whistleblowers. One example was where the organization had commissioned an independent review into an alleged bullying culture at a specific department in response to a whistleblowing concern. The review had not found a bullying culture. Nevertheless, the whistleblower continued to blow the whistle to the regulator and the media.

As reported in a previous section, a number of our interviewees reported that they were restricted by law from communicating details about what the investigation had found and what sanctions were taken against wrongdoers. In most cases, all they could communicate was a vague, standardized message thanking the whistleblower and ensuring them their information had been very helpful. These restrictions seemed to reduce the agency of the speak-up operator in supporting trust:

> *Where [does a whistleblower] get the trust from that it has been dealt with properly? [...] Obviously if the activity that has been complained about were to continue then that would be evidence that it hasn't been dealt with properly. [...] But you won't get detail about what action has been taken against an individual. And invariably, where there is something of substance that has been investigated and found to be true.*
>
> *Get it wrong: everyone knows; get it right: no one hears, so it still doesn't reinforce that it is a safe method of communication.*

Perhaps this is the phase in the whistleblowing process where the whistle-blower is required to make the biggest 'leap of faith' or suspension. This is because outcomes cannot be communicated in detail, and sanctions against a wrongdoer are not always visible. There is little to nothing for the whistleblower to cogni-tively interpret. A couple of our interviewees had developed strategies to facilitate the whistleblower's suspension, and thus maintain trust.

By responding quickly and communicating frequently, asking the whistle-blower further questions, speak-up operators hoped whistleblowers would per-ceive the follow-up and the investigation as serious processes, and would hence be able to accept a vague communication about the outcome of the investigation or even that the investigation had not found wrongdoing. Speak-up operators too had to make a 'leap of faith' here, so much so that sometimes all they could do was to hope that the whistleblower would not raise their concern externally with a regula-tor. This was especially the case where a whistleblower had created a phony email account to disclose information but never seemed to check that account after this.

What becomes clear from all this is that the speak-up process involves trust relationships between a number of actors.

Our findings suggest that trust relationships around speak-up arrangements cannot be understood as dyadic. The speak-up operator will not solely facilitate trust between the whistleblower on the one hand, and the wrongdoer and line manager on the other hand. Rather, the speak-up operator will seek to establish trust with the whistleblower by establishing favorable expectations with regard to the competence and intention of the speak-up operator to stop the wrongdoing and shield the whistleblower from retaliation by the wrongdoer or line manager.

In a sense, we can see this as trust repair at the organizational level.[69] One might argue that a person who lacks trust to raise a concern about wrongdoing directly with the wrongdoer, and who has been ignored by the line manager (or even experienced retaliation) will have lost trust in the organizational competence and intention to take their concern seriously. In these cases—where trust towards the organization is 'dead'—a whistleblower might disclose to a regulator or the media.[70] Thus, the whistleblower trusts the external recipient more because there is a lack of trust towards the organization. This is why we called this 'prey-trust'. It is as if the whistleblower has a need to trust someone, an inherent need to 'leap' somewhere, and 'leaps' to the regulator or media when the 'gorge' of trust towards the organization has become too wide.[71] Eberl et al.[72] studied trust repair, taking more than two actors into account. In their reconstruction of trust repair, at Siemens after a corruption scandal, they show that the intervention by Siemens was successful in repairing trust with external stakeholders but not with internal stakeholders. Our own research shows a more complex situation. Trust repair between a whistleblower and the organization does not involve trust repair between the internal actors (whistleblower, wrongdoer, and line manager), as it happens in a context of competing for the whistleblower's trust between the organization, the regulator, and the media. As such, insights into how speak-up operators seek to establish their trustworthiness towards the whistleblower is inextricably connected to maintaining trust with other internal stakeholders, that is, potential wrongdoers, managers at various levels, and potential future whistleblowers.

Before we discuss how to navigate the pitfalls, it is helpful to recap. How do speak-up operators seek to establish trust with the whistleblower? From our research we learn that this takes place in different phases involving: (1) establishing trust so that the whistleblower raises the concern through an internal rather than external disclosure; (2) maintaining trust during the investigation; (3) maintaining trust after the investigation and action taken towards the wrongdoing. In each of these phases speak-up operators provide different signals to facilitate interpretation and suspension by whistleblowers as shown in Table 4.5. In the first phase, speak-up operators signal secrecy (anonymity and confidentiality) and independence. In the second phase, speak-up operators need to win time. An investigation can take more than a couple of months, during which there is a risk that the whistleblower turns to the regulator or the media. Speak-up operators try to reproduce

TABLE 4.5 Strategies for building trust

Stage of Trust	Strategies		
Establishing trust	Empathizing with the whistleblower	Meet face-to-face with the whistleblower	Emphasize the independence of the compliance office
Maintaining trust	Be clear on limitations	Gain credibility to both organization and whistleblower	Communicate as much as possible with whistleblower— respond quickly and frequently
Maintaining trust after the investigation and action taken	Communicate outcome as much as possible to wider organization, e.g. intranet blog.		

trust by signaling that the investigation is making progress by asking the whistle-blower further questions about the wrongdoing. In the third phase, speak-up operators need the whistleblower to trust that there has been as investigation, that the wrongdoing has stopped, and that sanctions were taken against the wrongdoer. However, typically, none of this can be communicated. Whilst reproducing trust in this phase remains crucial—the whistleblower could still make a further external disclosure—speak-up operators have little to nothing to signal beyond this stage.

Hence, our study of trust throughout the speak-up process provides is a good example of how trust is continuously reproduced.[73] Laan et al.[74] studied how successive cycles of interactions produced increasing trust in the relationships between clients and contractors in the construction industry. What our research suggests is that reproducing trust does not necessarily become easier as the process progresses. Indeed, we found that trust tended to increasingly depend on 'bigger leaps of faith'. This was caused by factors both internal and external to the trust work itself. When whistleblowers trust speak-up operators and disclose information to them, they have expectations about their anonymity or about how the speak-up operator will maintain their confidentiality, and shield them from retaliation. Speak-up operators often induce this expectation through, for example, emphasizing their 'independence', or by secretly meeting with the whistleblowers. Such signals can form concrete expectations by the whistleblower that speak-up operators have moral obligations towards them[75] but they can also act as obstacles for reproducing trust after the disclosure is made. External factors hindering the reproduction of trust include legal and practical restrictions the speak-up operator faces with regard to communicating the outcome of the investigation. All the speak-up operators we interviewed acknowledged that privacy regulation (France and Spain were mentioned as being among the strictest) prevents them from providing details about the findings of an investigation into the wrongdoing, or about sanctions taken against a wrongdoer. Where concerns are raised anonymously, speak-up operators face the practical restriction that they cannot even communicate vague reassurances that the whistleblowing was helpful.

In terms of the competition between internal speak-up operators and external recipients for winning and maintaining the trust of the whistleblower, the moment when the investigation has produced findings—known to the speak-up operator but not to the whistleblower—is perhaps the most difficult stage in the speak-up process in terms of reproducing trust. In this final phase the agency of speak-up operators to provide signals for interpretation are limited, and hence they can only hope whistleblowers will make the 'leap of faith' needed to reproduce trust. Speak-up operators have to rely on 'the grapevine'—upon word-of-mouth—and in this sense speak-up operators themselves have to make a 'leap of faith' that the whistleblower will not further disclose to an external recipient. Nevertheless, there are theories about how such organizational 'word-of-mouth' is shaped, and our research provides clues about how to do this in the context of speak-up arrangements. We turn to this in the next section.

FACILITATORS OF RESPONSIVENESS

A climate of silence is characterised by the perception that speaking up is futile and risky, as detailed by Morrison and Milliken's influential work. This differs from a culture of silence, as discussed in Chapter 3 slightly, in that a 'culture of silence' involves more explicit barriers to speaking up. Such a climate is formed through an interactive process of collective sense making, in which salient events are exaggerated and generalized.[76] Collective sense making is a process of story-telling and other verbal interactions, through which people come to have a shared understanding of a situation without necessarily having experienced that situation. One interviewee at the bank stressed the symbolic importance of visible responsiveness for collective sense-making, in a rather extreme way:

> *What's been done and where's the body, where's that symbolic thing—I always talk about symbolism—Somebody's thrown off the fourth floor because they did the wrong thing. Leave the body there for a while. Everybody'll get it. (Bank interviewee B)*

Whilst management is limited in its ability to demonstrate responsiveness due to the reasons mentioned earlier, not all actions against wrongdoers are invisible. Some of the organizations in our research seemed to assume there were enough of these visible cases to create a shared perception that the organization was responsive to speak-up concerns. At the engineering company, word-of-mouth communication of visible responses among staff was relied on to create a shared perception of responsiveness.

From time to time, if somebody does the wrong thing, he or she has to leave the company, and everybody knows it [...] they hear it, grapevine, that this or that person had to leave the company because of bad behaviour, because of stealing something, because of doing something with corruption, and so on. (Engineering company interviewee D)

It's not difficult to go to internet to see that the company also terminated the contract of the former CEO because of our wrongdoing. And then it's quite easy for every single employee from the company in this country to understand that the rules apply to everyone and the system works. It's not a thing that I need to emphasise very much here. (Engineering company interviewee E)

Management needs to find indirect ways of creating a more general perception of responsiveness. We now elaborate on different ways in which the organizations we studied attempted to do this.

Always Be as Responsive as You Can

At the NHS Trust an attempt to be responsive is made by publishing answers to voiced questions or concerns where no other person is accused of wrongdoing, on the intranet visible to all staff. Rather than relying on mere word-of-mouth or hoping that some cases are salient enough, the NHS Trust tries to maximise the opportunities to form a shared perception of effective organizational responsiveness. Research literature notes that a supportive organizational culture is needed for whistleblowing or voicing concerns about wrongdoing. However, the literature remains vague as to the factors that create such a culture.[77] Our research suggests that because organizations have only limited agency to be responsive to employee voice, it is important for management to be as responsive as possible even where a speak-up channel is used to voice concerns that do not lead to investigations or sanctions. Without a proper speak-up arrangement, these concerns would be neglected. Effective speak-up arrangements however see these concerns as an excellent opportunity to demonstrate their responsiveness, as they are not bound by legal limitations and can thus communicate the response openly within the organization.

The NHS Trust also had positive experiences with involving an employee who had raised the concern, in developing a solution to the problem. It must be noted that the concern in question related to an operational matter rather than a compliance-related issue. Including the employee who had made the speak-up in the team that developed and implemented a solution to the problem had generated positive collective sense-making. We believe organizations should not underestimate the importance of such events for effective speak-up arrangements. In our secondary interview data we found instances in which unresolved operational concerns had either grown further into problems harming clients and the public interest, and had made whistleblowers escalate their concerns to regulators and the press.

Some of the speak-up operators we interviewed believed that a number of successful whistleblowing cycles lasting for close to ten years had created some kind of generalized trust. They believed others no longer saw them as 'police' but rather as 'trusted advisers'. This is an example of what Möllering[78] calls 'trust as becoming'. Other speak-up operators, however, were still waiting for such a generalized trust to take shape. They felt that confronting wrongdoers still triggered reactions that were too emotional or were taken as personal attacks. Interviewees used wording such as 'it has to be in the mechanisms' and even compared it to playing a rugby game. What this suggests is that the individual 'becoming' as a trustee coincides with a collective 'becoming'. Perceiving someone differently—for instance, as police versus adviser—entails a different interpretation of what that person is doing, and why they are doing it. This facilitates different expectations—in terms of the changing rules of the 'game'. If speak-up arrangements work in the sense that trust is reproduced throughout successive cycles, then generalized trust emerges. However, in the cases where such generalized trust seemed to have emerged, this did not necessarily include trust between the person witnessing the wrongdoing and the wrongdoer. To the extent that a notion of generalized trust was referred to in the interviews, it was with regard to the functioning of the speak-up arrangements in the organization, more precisely, in terms of the relations between whistleblower and speak-up operator, and between speak-up operator and wrongdoer/line manager. The relation between the whistleblower and the wrongdoer/line manager remained constantly as one characterized by the lack of trust.

USING SPEAK-UP DATA

Speak-up arrangements integrate voice channels through centrally registering and tracking employee concerns. In theory this allows top management and board members to assess how receptive to employee voice is the culture at various locations and levels within the organization. The term 'voice culture' refers to the set of shared beliefs about how safe and effective it is to voice a concern. We find that our sample organizations are at various stages in making use of this additional data.

Pattern Recognition

Whilst the engineering company and the hospital carried out pattern recognition to spot potential issues underlying unsubstantiated concerns, the other organization was still discussing whether a concern voiced informally at local level should be registered as a 'speak-up'. A consistent finding across the cases however was that top management did have the intention of using data from the speak-up arrangement to steer management responses to voice at different levels. Currently, most of the organizations in our research reported numbers to board level, and outcomes of investigations into alleged wrongdoing to top management.

We simply report on facts. The more we report on these, it's down for management to learn based on the work that we do. It's down to management at senior level to say, 'Look, enough's enough,' and then send that message down, and then reiterate about the speak-up policy. (Bank interviewee MF)

The engineering company went further in this by also communicating and following up potential issues from the pattern recognition.

Data for Training Purposes

Although speak-up cases could be used for training purposes, the organizations in our research were reluctant to do so. The reasons mentioned by the interviewees centred on confidentiality and keeping the whistleblower safe.

I can't work out a way to do it without the individuals who raise issues feeling a little bit compromised. (Bank interviewee Gi)

Whilst the speak-up operators in the engineering company sometimes used speak-up cases for training purposes, they preferred making the 'back-office' process of what happens with an employee concern the central message, emphasising independence of investigation and follow-up.

Publishing Aggregated Speak-up Data

Another way in which the speak-up data could be used is by publishing aggregated numbers of reports from the speak-up arrangement in the annual report. Two of the organizations in our research had signed up to the 'First100' campaign launched by Public Concern at Work in the UK. When organizations sign up, they pledge to implement a speak-up arrangement in line with the Code of Practice published by the Whistleblowing Commission.[79] This commits them to publish speak-up numbers in their annual report. However, these organizations had signed up to First100 too recently to have experience with reporting speak-up numbers publicly. In research that *Public Concern at Work* conducted on initial experiences of the First100 signatories,[80] one of the surveyed organizations reported that they had received questions from investors with regard to the types of concerns employees had raised through the speak-up arrangement. Management had found this a positive interest from investors. The organization nevertheless remained 'nervous' about reporting numbers publicly through the annual report, fearing it might trigger an influx of questions from other stakeholders. Coincidentally, one of the organizations in our research that was not a First100 signatory does publish aggregated numbers from its speak-up arrangement in its annual report. A speak-up operator from that organization felt that, on the one hand, this was risky because sometimes the number are misinterpreted:

Sometimes we receive questions from journalists who want to have more detailed numbers. You cannot compare the incoming cases of one period, let's say one year or one quarter, with the disciplinary measures and the closing of the cases, because sometimes complex investigations take more than half a year or more than one year in total. Therefore, the numbers do mostly not refer to the same cases, they are just stating the in- and output of cases without saying anything about how much is still ongoing within the compliance organization. If we in one year have an incoming number of 100 cases and in parallel to that outline disciplinary measures in or closing of 60 cases, that does not mean we are only handling 60 of the 100 cases. We may very well have 40 open cases which are passing on to the next quarter or the next year. (Engineering company interviewee 2)

This interviewee nevertheless also saw benefits of reporting number publicly:

I think, from that intense culture of internal transparency, but as well of pride concerning the effective first steps already taken the motivation arose to put the figures in the annual report [. . .] By publishing, we promote transparency, demonstrating that the compliance system you've seen is alive and working, and that there are cases being investigated. (Engineering company interviewee 2)

As more organizations start to publish data from their speak-up arrangement, a voluntary standard of what and how to report these numbers could mitigate the risks of misreading the information and other first-mover disadvantages with regard to increased transparency.[81] Such a standard might also be helpful for the further development of best practices in designing and implementing speak-up arrangements.

BRINGING IT ALL TOGETHER: A MODEL FOR DEVELOPING SUSTAINABLE SPEAK-UP SYSTEMS

Based on these insights we propose a model for sustainable speak up systems, depicted in Figure 4.4. The key success factors for operating speak-up systems, identified in our empirical research, are independence, responsiveness and time. The independence of the speak-up recipient is key. This is because employees are more likely to speak up to a recipient that is removed from the wrongdoing. In addition, responsiveness is essential; employees must perceive that their report is being acted on for speak-up arrangements to work. There are sometimes barriers to

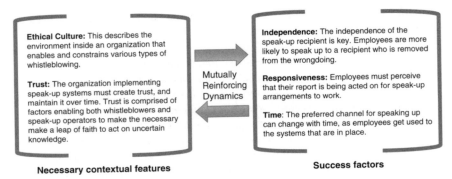

Necessary contextual features   **Success factors**

FIGURE 4.4   Sustainable Speak-up Systems: A Model

how responsive the organization can be, as we have described. Finally the preferred channel for speaking up can change with time as employees get used to the systems that are in place.

Combining this with insights from earlier research studies, it is clear that to enable independence, to enhance responsiveness and to support speak-up systems over time, two contextual features are necessary. An ethical culture in the organization, and a strong atmosphere of trust, are both required. Kaptein's work on ethical culture describes the environment inside an organization that enables and constrains various types of whistleblowing. He shows how culture has an impact on how employees speak up, and to whom.[82]

Through our empirical analysis we add trust to this vital aspect. Trust needs to be created in the organization implementing such systems but also maintained over time. For successful speak-ups, whistleblowers and speak-up operators have to make a 'leap of faith' and act on uncertain knowledge. Strategies for creating this trust include empathy with the whistleblower, and providing a choice of interfaces for the whistleblower to choose from. Adding to this, strategies for maintaining trust include communications regarding investigations that emerge from speak-ups and the relevant steps, along with operator independence. The implementation of these strategies must account for the fact that the success factors of effective speak up and the organizational contextual factors that enhance them are mutually constitutive. This means that the presence of each supports and reinforces the other. Increased responsiveness and the introduction of independent channels build trust, for example, which in turn enhances the success of speak up practices.

CONCLUSION

In this chapter we have drawn on our empirical work and the literature to explore how people speak up, as well as what challenges and expectations speak-up arrangements face. We began with Kaptein's research on ethical workplaces, highlighting that even ethical organizations need whistleblowing policies, precisely because some of their ethical virtues will lead employees either to remain silent—potentially losing their commitment—or to blow the whistle outside the organization. We then presented research from various authors that shows whistleblowing is a protracted process, and whistleblowers usually speak up more than once, to increasingly independent recipients. Next, we used two axioms from Watzlawick's communication theory tho show how the lack of a perceived response can actually be a response to a whistleblower. This draws attention to some of the challenges of operating speak up systems that we identified in our empirical research: Independence, responsiveness and time. We found that the independence of the recipient is key, as employees are more likely to speak up to a receipient that is removed from the wrongdoing. Additionally responsiveness was key, as employees must perceive that their report is being acted on for speak-up arrangements to work. There are sometimes barriers to how responsive the organization can be, as we identified in our empirical work. When anonymous concerns are raised, it is hard to communicate to the whistleblower that thier concern is being taken seriously. Additionally, legal issues may prevent organizations from publicising the actions that they have taken to correct the wrongdoing. Even when organizations do act, if the response is invisible, such as when an employee is reprimanded, it may be difficult to communicate this back to the whistleblower. Finally, the preferred channel for speaking up can change with time, as employees get used to the systems that are in place.

We stress the importance of trust in overcoming these barriers, and offer strategies for creating and maintianing trust, as well as tips to facilitate responsiveness. Key to this is keping and using data on the number of speak-ups that are received in the organization. In the following chapter we present recommendations for how to put all of this into practice.

ENDNOTES

1. Kaptein (2011).
2. Kaptein (2011).
3. Ibid.
4. Ibid.
5. Kaptein (2011: 520).
6. Kaptein (2011: 521).
7. Kaptein (2011).
8. Smith and Brown (2008); Roberts et al. (2011).
9. Skivenes and Trygstad (2010).
10. Skivenes and Trygstad (2010: 1077).
11. Lewis and Vandekerckhove (2015).
12. Rothschild and Miethe (1999).
13. Ibid: 119.
14. Rothschild and Miethe (1999: 119–120).
15. Donkin et al. (2008)

16. Ibid.
17. Public Concern at Work (2013).
18. Donkin et al. (2010).
19. Ibid.
20. Rothschild and Miethe (1999).
21. Vandekerckhove and Phillips (2017).
22. PCAW (2013).
23. Donkin et al. (2010).
24. Vandekerckhove et al. (2014).
25. Watzlawick et al. (1967).
26. PCAW (2013).
27. Weiskopf and Tobias-Mersch (2016).
28. Lovell (2002).
29. PCAW (2013); Rothschild and Miethe (1998).
30. Bird and Bird (1996).
31. de Graaf (2016).
32. Anechiarico and Jacobs (1996).
33. Anechiarico and Jacobs (1996: 69).
34. Langenberg (2008); Vandekerckhove and Langenberg (2012).
35. Harlos (2001).
36. Holtzhausen (2009); Near and Miceli (1985).
37. Binikos (2006).
38. Milliken et al. (2003).
39. Vandekerckhove and Phillips (2017).
40. Bachman et al. (2015); Laan et al. (2011); Möllering (2001, 2006, (2013); Nooteboom (1996, 2006); Saunders et al. (2014).
41. Nooteboom (2006).
42. Kenny (2015).
43. Vandekerckhove and Phillips (2017).
44. Roberts et al., 2011.
45. Klaas et al. (2012: 324).
46. Morrison and Milliken (2000).
47. Vandekerckhove, Brown, and Tsahuridu (2014).
48. Harlos (2001); Morrison and Milliken (2000).
49. DLA Piper (2017).
50. Möllering (2013).
51. Nooteboom (1996).
52. Adobor (2005).
53. Jagd (2010).
54. Möllering (2013).
55. Lane and Bachmann (1998); Kramer (1999).
56. Fotaki (2014).
57. Möllering (2001: 404).
58. Möllering (2001).
59. McEvily (2011).
60. Möllering (2013).
61. Möllering (2013: 291).

62. Möllering (2013).
63. Fotaki et al. (2015).
64. Möllering (2013).
65. Mollering (2013: 294).
66. Moberly and Wiley (2011); Vandekerckhove and Commers (2004).
67. Möllering (2001).
68. Ibid.
69. Gillespie and Dietz (2009).
70. Kenny (2015).
71. cf. the metaphor used in Möllering (2001).
72. Eberl et al (2015).
73. Möllering (2013).
74. Laan et al. (2011).
75. Möllering (2001).
76. Morrison and Milliken (2000).
77. Near and Miceli (1992).
78. Möllering (2013).
79. PCAW (2015).
80. Ibid.
81. Vandekerckhove, Fotaki, Kenny, Humantito, and Ozdemir Kaya (2016).
82. See also Roberts et al. (2011).

CHAPTER 5

Speak-up Procedures: A Guide for Professionals

In this chapter, we present a practical guide for professionals that is based on our analysis of relevant theories as well as our empirical research. In our empirical analysis, the key issues that emerged were ethical culture, trust building, effective communication and the importance of employee voice. In our analysis of the extant literature, we identified several key theories that can be linked together to create a framework for practical use (see Appendix for summary of key theories and how they link). The recommendations that follow are derived from this framework, and represent a novel way of understanding speak-up arrangements.

(The following, with some minor updates, is taken with permission from Vandekerckhove et al. (2016), Designing and Implementing Effective Speak-up Arrangements. *Report to ACCA, developed from the research project* Effective speak-up Arrangements for Whistle-blowers, *which was carried out between September 2015 and June 2016 and funded by ACCA and ESRC.)*

EXECUTIVE SUMMARY

This chapter is meant to serve as a practical guide on how to design and implement effective speak-up arrangements. It is based on a synthesis of best practice from our comparative research presented in Chapter 3, which included a healthcare organization (an NHS Trust in the UK), a multinational bank, and a multinational engineering company; and an extensive analysis of existing literature. In addition, supplementary empirical material from a study of speak-up arrangements at central government in Southeast Asia was utilized.

In what follows, we give illustrative examples alongside clear practical recommendations.

The guide:

- Lists benefits of operating effective speak-up arrangements.
- Introduces different types of speak-up channels, their strengths and weaknesses.
- Provides detailed recommendations concerning how to design and operate speak-up arrangements.
- Identifies the challenges an implementing organization may face in due process.
- Suggests strategies that can be adopted to address these challenges.

BENEFITS OF EFFECTIVE SPEAK-UP ARRANGEMENTS:

1. For the Organization
   1.1 Prevents financial loss: Both public and private sector organizations can save money by implementing effective speak-up arrangements. Recent research carried out in 40 countries showed that 40% of the 5,000-plus firms studied had suffered serious economic crimes resulting in an average of over $3 million each in losses.[1] Of these crimes, 43% were exposed by whistleblowers. This means that whistleblowing was more effective than all other measures for preventing wrongdoing combined: corporate security, internal audits and law enforcement.
   1.2 Prevents reputational loss: Workers who voice their concern can help to prevent the dysfunctional behaviour that leads to reputational losses if there are robust response systems in place. In their absence, unresolved operational concerns lead whistleblowers to escalate their concerns to regulators and the press, as was seen in many high profile cases in the health sector including the UK's NHS. Financial services whistleblowers emerged in the aftermath of the 2008 financial crisis to highlight the wrongdoing that had taken place in their well-known banks.[2]
   1.3 Saves time and money on legal battles: Legal costs relating to whistleblowing disputes can be significant for both parties involved. Whistleblowing provides organizations the opportunity to address wrongdoing at an earlier stage. This prevents loss of time, money and effort in protracted legal battles. US whistleblowing advocate Tom Devine at the *Government Accountability Project* describes the detrimental effects that this can have on organizations.[3]
   1.4 Creates organizational trust: Three of the organizations we studied had introduced their speak-up arrangements in response to a crisis of trust. In the engineering company this crisis was triggered by wrongdoing

involving the organization, which led to media attention, police intervention and regulatory sanctions. In the NHS Trust regulators carried out inspections following a whistleblower concern raised with them. In the bank, the crisis in trust was triggered by scandals in the industry. All these organizations rebuilt trust by implementing speak-up arrangements. Compliance officers from the bank and the engineering company noted that the speak-up arrangements have changed employees' perception of their role from 'policing' to 'helping'.

2. **For the Employee**

  2.1 Prevents retaliation: Lack of procedures to receive and follow-up concerns raised by employees leads to exacerbated suffering and retaliation.[4] Research shows the vicious nature of retaliation that some whistleblowers can receive at the hands of colleagues, managers and wider society.[5] Even though laws have been introduced, it is difficult to effectively legislate against such responses. But speak up systems can lessen this effect.

  2.2 Makes raising concerns more effective: Proper arrangements for investigating and following up concerns allow for wrongdoing to be stopped at an early stage, so workers can continue to be committed to the organization and their work.

3. **For Society**

  3.1 Protects public interest: Our research shows instances in which unresolved operational concerns had grown further into problems harming clients and the public interest. Examples from many sectors including the BP whistleblowers who could have prevented the Gulf oil spill, or the Piper Alpha disaster, internal auditors in Indonesia,[6] the NHS whistleblowers in Mid-Staffordshire Foundation Trust and others, demonstrate how harm to the public and costs to the companies could have been prevented if whistleblowers' disclosures had been heeded.

  3.2 Maintains trustworthy institutions and organizations: Responding to internal whistleblowing by correcting the wrongdoing and keeping the whistleblower unharmed creates institutions and organizations that can be trusted.

RECOMMENDATIONS

This section offers practical and detailed recommendations for organizations designing and operating speak-up arrangements.

1. Offer a variety of speak-up channels.

Effective speak-up arrangements are a combination of channels through which employees can voice a concern involving.

- Informal channels
- Question channel.
- Key internal persons.
- Internal hotline.
- External hotline.
- External ombudsperson.
- External independent advice channel.
- IT-based channels.
- Email and Web applications.

Each of these channels has its own limitations. For example, their perceived accessibility exhibits differences depending on national culture and societal context. The extent to which any of these channels is used changes over time.

The engineering company we researched has operated a combination of speak-up channels for almost a decade. The management implemented these channels as part of an organizational overhaul of the compliance function. This function was centralized, given more independence, and grew tenfold. Initially the question channel was used the most because employees raised integrity-related questions through a Web interface. Subsequently more employees began raising concerns through the externally operated hotline. More recently, in most of the regions where the company operates, employees have turned to open and direct communication. Their experience shows that familiarity and positive experiences with one channel positively affects trust in other channels.[7]

These experiences show that providing a range of speak-up channels:

- Allows these channels to compensate for each other's limitations.
- Increases accessibility.
- Caters to various national, cultural and organizational preferences.

2. Involve more than one function in your speak-up arrangement.

We found that organizations with speak-up arrangements operated by more than one function are more responsive. Functions such as compliance and HR should liaise with each other through clear protocols in a coordinated manner. This creates a division of labour in which each function applies its specialism. At the bank we researched, for example, Strategic HR owns the speak-up arrangement and liaises with the special investigations unit (whose role is to oversee compliance). One function is to 'mantle' the voicing employee and follow up his or her well-being, and the other function investigates the potential wrongdoing. In the engineering firm, HR and the compliance work together on cases with both grievance and wrongdoing aspects, and all alleged wrongdoing is investigated by the compliance function.

We also noted that different functions within the speak-up arrangements can set the 'tone' and encourage employees to voice concerns. For example, the bank we researched moved the oversight of the speak-up arrangement from the compliance function to the HR function at group level. This widened the scope of concerns taken into account, and shifted the attitude from 'policing' to well-being and engagement. This arrangement was supported by an additional free and independent advice channel that provided information on how to raise a concern and how the law protects those that do. In the NHS Trust, the HR and the board focused mainly on employment and patient safety issues, and the Trust Local Counter Fraud Specialist and the Finance Department respond to concerns about fraud, bribery and corruption. By dividing the responsibilities and ensuring that reports to the incorrect channel are redirected, the Trust is able to show they are taking a wide array of concerns seriously. These policies positively affected trust.

3. Build trust through speak-up arrangements.

Trust is crucial in encouraging employees to speak-up. So, it is often assumed that you should build trust before implementing speak-up arrangements. Our research shows that effective speak-up arrangements can actually help your organization build trust. This process manifests itself through speak-up practices that evolve over time, and are supported by the independence of speak-up operators.

A crucial characteristic of channels that further trust is the level of independence of the speak-up operator. The perception of independence is based on speak-up operators' specialist role and rule-bound referrals (we use the term 'rule-bound referrals' for protocols and policies that specify rules for managers at different levels about how, when, and to whom within the organization a concern raised by an employee must be escalated). Where receiving and following-up speak-up concerns was central rather than marginal to their core job task, speak-up operators were able to:

- Keep focus on appropriate listening.
- Objectively evaluate the quality of investigations.
- Carry out and document end-to-end follow-up of concerns.
- Spot potential wrongdoing underlying concerns that seemed unsubstantial or unfounded at first sight.

For this research, it is vital to ensure that the speak-up operators are given the time and resources to practise this work.

4. Be responsive.

Effective speak-up arrangements involve robust systems to respond to concerns. Organizations must be as responsive as they can. They should explore whether employees who raised a concern can be included in developing a solution to the problem. This can increase trust in the effectiveness of the speak-up arrangement. It can be a valuable opportunity for positively changing collective understanding of transparency and affect individual employee behaviour.

Responsiveness needs to be well organized, clearly mandated, and adequately resourced. Follow-up activities must be planned and coordinated. Organizations should consider the following recommendations in order to build robust response systems:

- Responding: Research shows that at least half of the concerns raised through speak-up channels are not about wrongdoing (harm to the public interest, breach of regulation, or breach of organizational policy). Such concerns are often disregarded as 'employee grievances' or just a nuisance. In our research there were examples where the compliance function had initially referred a concern to the specialist HR speak-up operator because they believed it had no compliance-related content. When the HR officer looked into the matter however, issues were uncovered that had relevance for compliance but were not initially mentioned by the employee. Therefore, it is important to prepare your organization to respond to both grievance and wrongdoing-related concerns, for risk management purposes. Specialist speak-up operators tend to be more capable of identifying operational, people management-related, or compliance-related risks at an earlier stage.
- Investigation: As mentioned earlier, organizations should explore whether employees who raised a concern can be included in developing a solution to the problem. Seize the opportunity to increase trust. The NHS Trust that we studied provided a good example for this strategy. A staff member raised a concern related to an operational matter, which was not compliance-related. They formed a team to develop and implement a solution to the raised issue and included the voicing employee in the team. This proved to be a good opportunity for collective sense making.
- Intervention: Design your speak-up 'back office' to investigate and intervene with regard to different types of concern. Be ready to deal with employee concerns triggered by the external environment. Scandals in your sector, country or at a global scale can change the attitude towards speaking up. A Latin American branch of the engineering company, for example, experienced a sudden increase in speak-up events following a scandal that involved a publicly owned company operating in a different sector. A speak-up operator from the engineering company believed that the surge in the complaints they received resulted from the changing public attitude towards speaking up.

5. Be aware of the barriers to responsiveness.

Being responsive does not guarantee being perceived as such. Inability to share the results of an investigation due to legal limitations or not having the contact information of an anonymous whistleblower may lead an organization to be perceived as irresponsive. Nevertheless, it is the perceived response rather than the real response that matters for creating trust, which encourages employees to raise concerns in the future. For this reason it is important for managers and speak-up operators to understand barriers to being perceived as responsive and to develop strategies that address them. Failure to do so may create a culture of silence or lead whistleblowers to escalate their concerns to regulators and the press. These barriers include the following:

- Anonymous Concerns: Concerns are often raised anonymously for fear of retaliation. Communicating back to someone who voiced concern anonymously is difficult, if not impossible. Anonymous speak-ups often occur through purposely made email accounts, for example, whistle333@hotmail.com. These email accounts can be used to raise a concern but are not checked afterwards to see if there is a response. Therefore, the speak-up operator's efforts to communicate back inevitably fail. An added problem is encountered when additional information about the alleged wrongdoing is sought.
- Legal Limitations: Privacy and data protection regulations limit what can be communicated about an investigation or outcome. Conveying details can inhibit legal proceedings against a wrongdoer. Therefore, speak-up operators often can only provide limited and vague information about investigations and outcomes. This may leave the voicing employee with the impression that their concern is not taken seriously.
- Invisibility of the Response: Sanctions against a wrongdoer are not always visible to other organizational members. For example, a minor wrongdoing might be sanctioned by a reprimand or a formal warning. Invisibility of sanctions is an added barrier in demonstrating responsiveness.

6. Develop strategies to circumvent barriers to responsiveness.

Organizations can adopt various strategies to circumvent barriers to responsiveness. Some of these strategies directly address the problems previously listed. Others aim to create a generalised perception of a responsive organization.

- Legal limitations: Speak-up operators should manage the expectations of voicing employees. To do so,
  - Give them an indicative timescale of follow-up activities.
  - Inform them of legal limitations that prevent you from providing a detailed response.
- Invisibility of Sanctions: Some organizations rely on word-of-mouth amongst employees in making sanctions visible. A more strategic approach is to create a generalised perception of a responsive organization by:

- o Communicating widely about concerns that were not related to wrongdoing.
- o Engaging with the voicing employee in finding a solution to the problem.
- o Reporting on the aggregated speak-up events: The NHS Trust we researched published answers to voiced questions or concerns where no other person is accused of wrongdoing, on the intranet visible to all staff.
- o Being responsive to concerns that do not lead to investigations or sanctions: A supportive organizational culture is necessary in order to encourage whistleblowing. Because there are limits to organizations' responsiveness, it is important for management to seize every opportunity to demonstrate responsiveness. Responses to concerns that do not lead to investigations or sanctions should be considered as such opportunities because the response can be openly communicated within the organization without breach of law.

7. Shape and coordinate attitudes to responding.

Organizations should continuously reinforce the message to managers at all levels that responding to concerns is part of their role. They should also restrict managers' discretion about how to respond to speak-up attempts. Giving a coherent and consistent response is crucial for building trust.

8. Involve third parties wherever possible.

Our research shows that involvement of third parties, such as unions, in the speak-up process is beneficial. There is typically no 'contracting' between a union and a company, and in this sense unions, like regulators, are not part of speak-up arrangements.[8] Theoretically, unions can give employees advice on how to raise a concern and even be a source of support. Our research shows however that this is not a common practice. Among the organizations we researched, only the NHS Trust explicitly lists this route.

9. Record all speak-up events.

Some concerns raised with speak-up operators will not lead to investigation or sanction. Such concerns, by themselves, may seem unimportant and not worth recording. However, recording all speak-up events is useful for:

- ■ Recognising patterns of concerns resulting from underlying problems: This helps identify and interfere with issues at an early stage. The speak-up data will strengthen the organization's risk management, beyond simply filtering for alleged wrongdoing worth investigating. Managers can use them to monitor risk cultures. In this sense, speak-up arrangements help organizations improve risk awareness and internal controls in proactive organizations.

■ Collecting data for training purpose: Speak-up cases can be used for training purposes. Concerns about the confidentiality and safety of the whistleblower often deter organizations from doing so. But strategies can be developed to use speak-up data without endangering confidentiality and whistleblower safety. The engineering company that we researched, for example, used speak-up data in developing their training programmes. Their message focused on the 'back-office' process of what happens with an employee concern and they emphasised independence of investigation and follow-up.

■ Monitoring speak-up cultures and most-used channels. There are often differences among departments or regions within the same organization in:

  ○ Frequency of speak-up events.
  ○ Channels used.
  ○ Types of concerns raised.

Managers and speak-up operators can use data on speak-up events to identify these differences and design their speak-up arrangements accordingly.

10. Report.

Organizations can use the speak-up data by publishing aggregated numbers of speak-up events in the annual report. They can also participate in the development of a standard for the public reporting of data from speak-up arrangements, with some efforts to support this evident in the UK for example.[9]

We have identified benefits for organizations in publicly reporting data:

■ Positive interest from investors: One organization that recently published speak-up results in its annual report notes that they had received questions from investors.[10] The queries were about the types of concerns employees had raised through the speak-up arrangement. The management interpreted this as positive interest from investors.

■ Internal transparency: An organization participating in our research publishes data publicly. A speak-up operator from that organization explains that reporting contributes to culture of internal transparency, and the pride in the effective first steps already taken motivated them to report.

Despite these benefits, organizations often hesitate in reporting numbers publicly through the annual report. They fear an influx of questions from other stakeholders and misinterpretation of the data. The aforementioned speak-up operator says:

Sometimes we receive questions from journalists who want to have more detailed numbers. You cannot compare the incoming cases of one period, let's say one year or one quarter, with the disciplinary measures and the closing of the cases, because sometimes complex investigations take more than half a year or more than one year in total. Therefore, the numbers do mostly not refer to the same cases, they are just stating the in- and output of cases without saying anything about how much is still ongoing within the compliance organization. If we in one year have an incoming number of 100 cases and in parallel to that outline disciplinary measures in or closing of 60 cases, that does not mean we are only handling 60 of the 100 cases. We may very well have 40 open cases which are passing on to the next quarter or the next year.' (Engineering company interviewee B)

There are risks associated with misinterpretation of data by uninformed parties, and other first-mover disadvantages following from increased transparency. But these can be mitigated as more organizations publish data from their speak-up arrangements. This is likely to lead to emergence of a voluntary standard of reporting on speak-up data. Such a standard can also contribute to further development of best practices in designing and implementing speak-up arrangements.

11. Consider national and organizational culture.

Culture is an important factor in the effectiveness of speak-up arrangements. The channels preferred and overall sense of receptiveness to voice, for example, are shaped by culture. When implementing a speak-up arrangement, it is important to understand the potentially difficult interactions between organizational and national cultures in order to develop an appropriate strategy.

The engineering multinational that we studied provides good insights into the impact of culture on effectiveness of speak-up arrangements. Their speak-up operators noticed that in some parts of the world people preferred to speak directly to a compliance officer. Calling a hotline or written communication through a web application did not appeal to them. The external ombudsperson was sometimes used to raise a concern in Germany, the Middle East, and Asian countries, but much less by employees in the UK, the United States, or Latin America.

The differences in speak-up channels preferred seems to be shaped by national culture. Yet, at times, organizational culture overrides national culture. The engineering multinational, for example, has a global expat strategy that ensures consistency across regions. Regional leaders are either nationals of the HQ-country or have several years of work experience with the company at the HQ.

Overcoming regional differences requires effort. As conveyed by an interviewee from Latin America, when the speak-up arrangement was initially rolled out, HQ had been clear enough on what structures, mandates, and reporting lines had to be implemented. However, it had taken a while for managers in Latin America to comprehend the rationale and the intended culture behind this.

12. Provide access in different languages.

For an effective speak-up arrangement, it is important to ensure accessibility in different languages especially in multinational organizations. The engineering company we studied provides a good example in this regard. Its web-based and hotline speak-up channels are available in the languages of all the countries in which it operates. It is telling that Latin American employees voiced their concern via these channels instead of the external ombudsperson because they assumed she would not speak Portuguese. On the other hand, having a shared conversational language (French) provided employees in the Maghreb and West Central African countries the chance to voice a concern directly to compliance officers. These examples show that provision of channels in local languages contributes to success of speak-up arrangements.

ENDNOTES

1. Devine (2012).
2. Francis (2013); Kenny (2019).
3. Devine and Massarrani (2011).
4. Alford (2001); Devine and Maassarani (2011).
5. Bjørkelo (2013); Mesmer-Magnus and Viswesvaran (2005); Rehg et al. (2008).
6. Fotaki and Humantito (2015).
7. Nooteboom, B. (2006).
8. There is, however, literature that argues unions should be part of speak-up arrangements. See Lewisand Vandekerckhove (2015); Vandekerckhove, James, and West (2013); Lewis and Vandekerckhove (2018).
9. See Public Concern at Work's 'First100' campaign, in which organizations pledge to implement a speak-up arrangement in line with the Code of Practice published by the Whistleblowing Commission, committing to publish their speak-up figures in their annual reports. Two of the organizations in our research are participants of the 'First100' campaign in the UK. However, these organizations had signed up to First100 too recently to have experience with reporting speak-up numbers publicly.
10. As reported in Public Concern at Work's research into its First 100 companies.

CHAPTER 6

Conclusions

In writing this book, we set out to accomplish two goals. We wanted to add to the existing academic research by exploring speak-up arrangements from the perspective of those that implement and operate them, and we wanted to provide practical advice for practitioners by making recommendations on best practice that emerged from the research. In this chapter, we will summarize our contributions in both of these areas. First, we return to the existing literature on whistleblowing, speak-up arrangements, as well as wider themes in organization studies and employee voice to highlight how this book has added to knowledge in these areas. Second, we review our empirical work, and revisit what we now know about speak-up arrangements. Third, we examine the framework we propose for understanding speak-up arrangements. This framework includes the themes of independence, responsiveness and time, and best practices to overcome challenges in these areas, which includes building trust, fostering an ethical culture in organizations, and learning from speak-up data. Finally, we re-iterate the practical relevance of the research, reviewing the recommendations for mangers and speak-up operators, providing a holistic understanding of speak-up arrangements in theory and practice. We begin with a review of the academic literature.

ACADEMIC LITERATURE

In Chapter 2 we discussed the issue of retaliation, which is a big risk for whistleblowers despite the fact that whistleblower protection is increasing. Not only is there more legislation being proposed and passed, but regulators are signalling that organizations are now responsible for creating cultures that encourage internal whistleblowing and are insisting that the organizations they regulate implement robust measures for the internal disclosure of information. Despite this, it is common for organizations to act out against the whistleblower. Reasons for retaliation vary; managers can feel deeply threatened by whistleblowers, both employers and co-workers can resort to reprisals to protect the reputation of specific colleagues or the organization itself, or retaliation can also be deployed as a means of deterring other potential whistleblowers in the organization. This last reason points to the power inequities between whistleblowers and organizations. These inequities are further uncovered by the types of retaliation that are deployed against the whistleblowers: demotion, decreased quality of working conditions, threats by senior staff, the allocation of menial duties to the whistleblower such that their job becomes degrading, harassment, referral to psychiatrists, outright dismissal from work and prolonged legal challenges are all various ways that whistleblowers are penalised. Research has shown that this treatment has severe impacts on the whistleblower. Their mental and physical health suffers, their livelihood is destroyed as they have difficulties finding another job in their field and their relationships often break down. All this points to the need for effective speak-up arrangements that minimize the impact of speaking up on the person disclosing the information. The question of how to develop such procedures that are both safe and effective has not received much attention in the literature, so our exploration of speak-up arrangements is a new contribution to the field of organization studies.

Research suggests a close link between retaliation and ethical culture in organizations. To understand ethical cultures we presented research by Kaptein,[1] which sheds light on the ethical environment inside an organization that enables and constrains various types of whistleblowing. His work shows how culture has an impact on how employees speak up, and to whom. This points to the need for speak-up arrangements, which provides clarity and assurances to employees who may otherwise be silent. This complements research by Morrison and Milliken on the climate of silence (see Chapter 4), which is formed through an interactive process of collective sense making, in which salient events are exaggerated and generalized. Additionally, other researchers on silence have found that the primary reasons behind the pervasiveness of silence are organizations' failure to investigate claims, retaliation against voicing employees, social isolation of voicing employees from colleagues, and gagging clauses.[2] Although useful, Kaptein's study, like others in the field of whistleblowing, treats speaking up as a static event. We have highlighted in this book recent empirical research that shows whistleblowing is a process, with whistleblowers seeking increasingly more independent recipients to disclose to if the issue they report is not resolved after the first speak-up. This research shows that most whistleblowers speak up at least two times, and that they do so internally before they go to external recipients. This brings internal and external whistleblowing to the fore, and while these have traditionally been researched as separate and somewhat opposite acts, the general consensus is that they are part of the same whistleblowing process. Nearly all external speak-ups were raised internally first. If effective speak-up arrangements were in place, organizations would be better able to prevent external whistleblowing. It is generally accepted that wrongdoing in organizations should be stopped or corrected as early as possible, because this is in the interest of both organization and society. This obviously requires organizational whistleblowing arrangements that succeed in encouraging workers to speak up through channels that allow organizational actors to respond to those concerns. Our research adds to this important area of research by examining some of the challenges that speak-up operators face when trying to implement arrangements that work in practice.

We also discuss the literature in employee voice as it relates to whistleblowing. Research in this field has split into three streams: employee relations, human resource management, and organizational behaviour. In the first two, articulation of voice represents a challenge to problematic forms of power within the structure and management of the organization. In the third, it represents an attempt to help out one's organization with the aim of improving it through addressing problems. Whistleblowing has usually been researched in the organizational behaviour stream, which sees it as prosocial behaviour meant to help the organization. In response, the critics from the employee relations and human resource management streams question this prosocial view, and allow for voice to be a way that employees speak up to challenge management. Recently, attempts have been made to synthesize the two views by shifting the focus away from the motivation of the whistleblower. This study continues in this trajectory by focusing on the channel and the response of speak-up operators and taking the stance that the motivation of the whistleblower is less important than the fact that speak-ups happen. We contribute to the literature with our recommendations for handling speak-up through processes that focus on the wrongdoing and not the motivation.

On a more theoretical note, we reviewed the research that likens whistleblowing to fearless speech (parrhesia), a concept from Ancient Greece that was developed by Michel Foucault. Fearless speech is understood as a spontaneous speaking truth to power where the speaker takes a risk in speaking out. This understanding brings out the political and ethical impacts of whistleblowing (Kenny et al., 2019)(see Box 2.8). This is important to research on speak-up arrangements because it highlights the need in organizational settings for the presence of an 'other' that is able to listen to the disruptive statement; without this, fearless speech's political impact is lost. This other is the recipient of the speak-up, and their responsiveness to the speak-up is key. Responsiveness is one of the key themes of the book, and our research adds to this debate by identifying the challenges to this responsiveness, even when the recipient is willing to act. One of the ways to overcome this challenge is to build trust in the organization.

An understanding of trust in organizations is also key to understanding whistleblowing. Trust is framed here as a process, complementing the process view of whistleblowing. In the literature on trust, Möllering considers the importance of expectations, experiences and leaps of faith in relation to how trust is created and maintained. Our research supports this view by taking the stance that, if we research ongoing interactions it is unreasonable to ignore that perceptions about past interactions, propensities towards opportunism, and possibilities of building trust are formed during these repeated interactions. We add to this literature with our empirical work that provides insights into how speak-up operators attempt to support trust between whistleblower, speak-up operator, and the organization.

One of the ways to facilitate trust is responsiveness. Responsiveness helps to reduce the culture of silence, although it is important to recognize that it is perceived responsiveness that counts. If the actions taken are invisible to the whistleblower, trust can be damaged even if actions are taken to correct the wrongdoing or discipline the wrongdoer. Our research points out some barriers to responsiveness, discusses how organizations try to overcome them, and also how speak-up arrangements can be a positive strategy in making sure responsiveness is visible.

Our research overall contributes to the literature in several areas, with both theoretical and practical implications. We highlight how research on speak-up arrangements contributes to research on retaliation, and how the speak-up arrangement can be implemented to minimize this, we contribute to research on whistleblowing as a process, and show how this poses challenges for speak-up operators and requires them to be visibly responsive. We contribute to the literature on whistleblowing and parrhesia by focusing on the response of speak-up operators and the challenges that they face in responding to disclosures, and we contribute to the literature on trust by showing how speak-up operators attempt to overcome obstacles and build trust in their organizations with regard to speak-up processes.

EMPIRICAL WORK

The second part of this book focuses on the comparative study of speak-up arrangements we conducted with organizations in the banking, engineering and healthcare sectors. Globally, a growing number of organizations are implementing speak-up arrangements, and speak-up reports are on the increase, but employees are not always satisfied with the arrangements that are being implemented. To help close this gap, we set out to identify best practice in speak-up design and operation. In Chapter 3 we analysed common types of wrongdoing, the state of speak-up systems in each sector, and how internal speak-up arrangements for each industry case sit against the political and economic context. We then outlined lessons learned and best practices based on evidence. First, we analysed the banking sector in which 'creative accounting', financial engineering and tax avoidance are the most pressing issues. The second case was from the engineering sector, where corruption has emerged in some big projects commissioned by public authorities, and where regulators are more prominent as health and safety are major concerns. Lastly, we analysed a public healthcare organization, where tackling threats to patient safety was at the top priority for speak-up operators. Here, highly regulated and complex organizational structures, operating under financial pressure and close public scrutiny, presented unique challenges. Common challenges and best practices emerged from the study.

In all of the sectors, political and economic pressure was a common challenge. The neoliberal view that the market will self-regulate contributed to organizational cultures that are overly tolerant of risk as long as profits are high and costs low. In the banking sector, fierce competition led to the use of new and highly complex financial instruments that challenged the legal and technological infrastructure as well as making risk analysis almost impossible for both banks and the regulators. In the engineering sector, the 2008 financial crisis resulted in redundancies, increases in workload, and decreases in wages. This led to intense competition and meant that companies had to cut costs and increase profits to survive. In addition to this, a substantial percentage of engineers were employed in multinationals that operate under multiple regulatory regimes, making regulation a difficult if not impossible task. In the health sector, a new consumerist model was introduced that was supposed to increase competition between NHS trusts. The effect of this was that quality of care was gradually replaced by consumer satisfaction as the measure of service quality, which resulted in insufficient monitoring and oversight of the quality of care. For all sectors, profit and efficiency was the main goal. Although this manifested in different forms of wrongdoing, the issues identified stemmed from the same source.

In our comparative research, common best practices emerged. In the banking organization various channels were offered for employees to speak up including: the line manager, internally operated hotline, dedicated email account, key persons and external advice channel. This provided increased accessibility as well as meeting the different needs of employees. Additionally, different functions were involved in operation of speak-up arrangements with clear protocols, which prevented speak-up operators from finding themselves in dual dependencies. The organization also demonstrated best practice in that no concern is turned down for being raised through the wrong channel. If an employee uses the grievance channel to raise a speak-up concern, they are signposted to the relevant function. Furthermore, we found that in this organization responsiveness was embedded in the speak-up process and formalised in the speak-up policy. Moreover, the bank had an external advice line that gave employees the opportunity to receive support and guidance from an independent body. This not only facilitated effective whistleblowing but also increased trust. Finally, the organization also documented all speak-up events.

The engineering firm also exhibited a number of best practices. First, it offered a variety of speak-up channels: the question channel, the externally operated hotline, internal key persons and the ombudsperson. The Web-based channel and the hotline were also offered in local languages, making them accessible to a wide range of employees. Second, it also involved more than one function in its speak-up arrangements, which liaised through clear protocols. Third, although the organization had separate arrangements for speak-up about wrongdoing and grievance, no concern was turned down for being raised through the wrong channel. Instead, employees were signposted to the relevant function. Fourth, there was evidence of building trust through speak-up arrangements. Fifth, responsiveness was formalized through procedures and protocols. Sixth, there was an effort to standardize and coordinate responsiveness through a global expat strategy. Seventh, external hotline and the external ombudsperson were available channels, which made it possible to raise concerns anonymously and provide confidentiality. Finally, speak-up events were documented, with the data used for risk monitoring and published in an annual report.

Lastly, in the NHS Trust, best practices that emerged were: first, a variety of channels were used. Although greater emphasis was put on informal channels in the policy, and these were more popular among staff, channels with varying degrees of formality, independence and anonymity are available. Second, it involved more than one function in its speak-up arrangements. Third, speak-up data was used to increase trust in the speak-up arrangement. Fourth, no concern was turned down for being raised through the wrong channel. Instead, they were redirected to the designated channel. Fifth, responsiveness was formalised through the whistleblowing policy. Sixth, there was awareness of the barriers to responsiveness and strategies were developed to circumvent them. Seventh, the Trust was working towards standardising and coordinating responsiveness across management. The policy registered managers' duty to respond promptly and appropriately. Eighth, the whistleblowing resource on the intranet provided information about the types of support offered by, and ways to contact, independent third parties. Finally, speak-up events were documented and the data was used to monitor attitudes to patient safety and staff engagement. It became clear that common best practices spanned across organizations, even though the context and the wrongdoing varied. These best practices are useful to practitioners who are operating or looking to implement speak-up arrangements, as they transcend sectoral and national boundaries. The findings also indicated there were limits to even the best speak-up arrangements, however, so we have developed a framework that helps practitioners understand and overcome barriers that exist in this area.

A FRAMEWORK FOR UNDERSTANDING SPEAK-UP ARRANGEMENTS

In reviewing the literature and the findings from our research, some key areas emerge. As important as speak-up arrangements are, they are worthless if no one uses them. Our research highlighted that an ethical culture and trust are also essential elements of an effective speak-up arrangement, and in turn speak-up arrangements can help to build trust and an ethical culture in an organization. Key to both of these are three themes that often pose challenges to speak-up operators: independence, responsiveness, and time.

Independence

Our findings from secondary data showed that a lack of independence of the speak-up operators lead to ineffective whistleblowing and a general distrust towards top management. Conversely, the speak-up operators that we interviewed felt that their level of independence from day-to-day operational matters gave them trust in their professionalism. The organizations we spoke to had different tactics for ensuring independence of the speak-up arrangement: using specialist speak-up operators, adopting rule-bound referrals, and utilising outsider independence. Each strategy helped build trust and make the speak-up arrangement more effective.

Responsiveness

The second element in our framework is responsiveness. Speak-up operators need to be perceived to respond to a disclosure of wrongdoing in order to build trust in the speak-up arrangement. If employees don't think that their concern is being dealt with, they will continue to raise it via other channels until they see that it is handled to their satisfaction. Our findings highlight that there are barriers to this perceived responsiveness, however, even if action is being taken. Barriers that we identified include anonymous concerns where there is no way to communicate actions taken back to the discloser, legal issues that prevent sensitive or personal information from being shared, and other actions that render the response invisible such as written or verbal warnings issued to the wrongdoers. Although barriers like these pose a challenge to responsiveness, we also identified strategies that the organizations used to overcome them. In one organization word-of-mouth communication of visible responses among staff was relied upon to make it known that the organization had acted on the concern raised. Additionally in the NHS Trust, answers to voiced questions or concerns where no other person is accused of wrongdoing were posted on the intranet and visible to all staff. By responding to the broad, operational level more serious concerns, the organization built up trust that other concerns would be addressed as well.

Time

Time is an important factor in ensuring that speak-up arrangements are effective, because trust and expectations change over time. When a speak-up arrangement is first implemented and employees are not as trusting of it, they will interact with it differently than they will after trust is established and they become comfortable with the processes. Additionally, speak-up operators' attitudes and perceptions can change with time as trust increases. In our research, whereas operators used to be 'police', after working on the arrangement for a period they felt they were perceived more as 'someone who can help'. This is important because it indicates that speak-up arrangements are not static, one-size-fits-all solutions that can be written and forgotten but, rather, steps in a process of trust-building in the organization.

The key point that emerged across sectors was that trust needs to be created and maintained in the organization. To do this, both whistleblowers and speak-up operators have to make a 'leap of faith' and act on uncertain knowledge. Strategies for creating this trust included empathizing with the whistleblower, simplifying the procedure so it was less intimidating, and having a choice of interfaces for the whistleblower to choose from, among others. Strategies for maintaining trust included signalling and communication that an investigation was going to happen and what the steps of an investigation include, and emphasizing the independence of the speak-up operator. These strategies, although not foolproof, helped the organizations we studied implement and develop processes that were effective. In summary, we frame our research on speak-up arrangements in terms of independence, responsiveness and time, and how these intertwine with trust and ethical culture. Using this approach we are able to not only contribute to existing research in these areas, but also provide a practical way for practitioners to understand and address the topic. It also allows for practical recommendations on how to implement and operate speak-up arrangements.

PRACTICAL RELEVANCE AND RECOMMENDATIONS

In the previous chapter, we compiled our analysis of the literature and of the empirical work we conducted, and we provided twelve recommendations for practitioners on how to design and implement effective speak-up arrangements. These recommendations are:

1. Offer a variety of speak-up channels.
2. Involve more than one function in your speak-up arrangement.
3. Build trust through speak-up arrangements.
4. Be responsive.
5. Be aware of the barriers to responsiveness.
6. Develop strategies to circumvent barriers to responsiveness.
7. Shape and coordinate attitudes to responding.
8. Involve third parties wherever possible.
9. Record all speak-up events.
10. Report.
11. Consider national and organizational culture.
12. Provide access in different languages.

Each of these recommendations is covered in depth in Chapter 5, but they are all related to the framework of independence, responsiveness and time that we articulated in the previous section (see Figure 4.4). By incorporating these elements into the implementation and operation of a speak-up arrangement, practitioners can make their processes more efficient and trustworthy, regardless of what sector they operate in.

To conclude, effective speak-up arrangements are crucial as new legislation and regulation is increasingly being implemented that mandates them, but they also have benefits for the organization, for the employee that makes a disclosure and for society as a whole. Our research builds upon the academic literature on trust, employee voice, ethical culture and whistleblowing more generally by providing empirical evidence on how speak-up arrangements work in practice. We also provide practical guidance for managers that are tasked with designing or implementing speak-up arrangements by looking at the challenges organizations have faced and the best practices they have implemented in this area. It is our hope that it is a useful resource to all that are interested in speak-up arrangements, whether they be academics, practitioners, or employees looking for guidance, and that speak-up arrangements continue to be implemented and improved to protect those that come forward to speak up about wrongdoing in organizations.

ENDNOTES

1. Kaptein (2011a, 2011b).
2. Heffernan (2012); Kenny (2014: 5); Tenbrunsel and Thomas (2015: 2).

Bibliography

ACFE. (2018). *Report to the Nations: 2018 Global Study on Occupational Fraud and Abuse*. Available at: https://s3-us-west-2.amazonaws.com/acfepublic/2018-report-to-the-nations.pdf [14 June 2018].

ACFE. (2010). *Report to the Nations on Occupational Fraud and Abuse*. Austin, TX: Association of Certified Fraud Examiners.

Adobor, H. (2005). Trust as sensemaking: The micro dynamics of trust in interfere alliances. *Journal of Business Research, 58*(3), 330–337.

Alford, C. F. (2001). *Whistleblowers: Broken lives and organizational power*. Ithaca, NY: Cornell University Press.

Alford, C. F. (2007) Whistle-blower narratives: The experience of choiceless choice. *Social Research 74*(1): 223–248.

Andrade, J. A. 2015 Reconceptualizing whistleblowing in a complex world. *Journal of Business Ethics, 128*(2), 321–335.

Anechiarico, F., & Jacobs, J. B. (1996). *The pursuit of absolute integrity: How corruption makes government ineffective*. Chicago: University of Chicago Press.

Angelides, P., Thomas, B., Born, B., Holtz-Eakin, D., Georgiou, B., Graham, B., … Wallison, P. J. (2011). *The Financial Crisis Inquiry Report: Final Report of the National Commission on the Causes of the Financial and Economic Crisis in the United States*. Washington, DC: U.S. Government Printing Office.

Armenakis, A. (2004). Making a difference by speaking out. *Journal of Management Inquiry, 13*(4), 355–362.

Aven, B. L. (2015). The paradox of corrupt networks: An analysis of organisational crime at Enron. *Organisation Science 26*(4), 980–996.

Bachmann, R., Gillespie, N. & Priem, R. (2015). Repairing trust in organizations and institutions: Toward a conceptual framework. *Organization Studies, 36*(9), 1123–1142.

Barbalet, J. (2009). A characterization of trust, and its consequences. *Theory & Society, 38*(4), 367–382.

Barry, M., & Wilkinson, A. (2016). Pro-social or pro-management? A critique of the conception of employee voice as a pro-social behaviour within organizational behaviour. *British Journal of Industrial Relations, 54*(2), 261–284.

BBC. (2018, 11 January). Luxleaks whistleblower Antoine Deltour has conviction quashed. Available at: http://www.bbc.co.uk/news/world-europe-42652161

Berwick, D. (2013). Independent Report: Berwick Review into Patient Safety. UK: Department of Health. Available at www.gov.uk/government/publications/berwick-review-into-patient-safety (accessed 20 March 2017).

Binikos, E. (2006). Sounds of silence: Organisational trust and decisions to blow the whistle. *South African Journal of Industrial Psychology, 34*(3), 48–59.

Bird, F. B., & Bird, F. B. (1996). *The muted conscience: Moral silence and the practice of ethics in business*. Greenwood Publishing Group.

BIS. (2015). *Whistleblowing: Guidance and Code of Practice for Employers*. UK: Department for Business Innovation and Skills. Available at www.gov.uk/government/publications/whistleblowing-guidance-and-code-of-practice-for-employers (accessed 20 March 2017).

Bjørkelo, B. (2013). Workplace bullying after whistleblowing: Future research and implications. *Journal of Managerial Psychology, 28*, 306–323.

Blogspot. (2015, 10 June). The ritual of the calling of an engineer. Available at: http://progress-is-fine.blogspot.com/2015/06/the-ritual-of-calling-of-engineer.html

Blueprint for Free Speech. (2018). Map. Available at: https://blueprintforfreespeech.net/en/whistleblowing-laws-map/ (accessed 14 June 2018).

Bolsin, S., Faunce, T., & Oakley, J. (2005). Practical virtue ethics: Healthcare whistleblowing and portable digital technology *Journal of Medical Ethics, 31*, 612–618.

Bolsin, S. (2012). Video Interview. *Insofar Media*. Available at: https://vimeo.com/54197275.

Boone, M. (2016, 5 August). The House for Whistleblowers Act has come into effect. *Leeman Verheijden Huntjens*. Available at: https://www.lvh-advocaten.nl/en/the-house-for-whistleblowers-act-has-come-into-effect-1116/

Boswell, P. (2010), Business Integrity Management Systems in the consulting engineering industry. In *Engineering: Issues, Challenges and Opportunities for Development* (pp. 195–196). Paris: UNESCO Publishing.

Bowers, J. Q. C., Fodder, M., Lewis, J., & Mitchell, J. (2012) *Whistleblowing: Law and practice*. Oxford: Oxford University Press.

Brown, A. J., & Donkin, M. 2008. Introduction. In A. J. Brown (Ed.), *Whistleblowing in the Australian public sector: Enhancing the theory and practice of internal witness management in public sector organizations* (pp. 1–24). Canberra: ANU E-Press.

Brown, A. J., Dozo, N., & Roberts, P. (2016, November). *Whistleblowing processes & procedures: An Australian & New Zealand snapshot*. Preliminary results of the Whistling While They Work 2 Project. Brisbane: Griffith University.

Burris, E. R. (2012). The risks and rewards of speaking up: Managerial responses to employee voice. *Academy of Management Journal, 55*, 851–875.

Burris, E., Rockmann, K., & Kimmons, Y. (2017) The value of voice to managers: Employee identification and the content of voice. *Academy of Management Journal, 60*(6), 2099–2125.

Burrows, J. (2001). Telling tales and saving lives: Whistleblowing – The role of professional colleagues in protecting patients from dangerous doctors. *Medical Law Review, 9*, 110–129.

Burrows, O., Low, K., & Cumming, F. (2015). Mapping the UK financial system. *Quarterly Bulletin*, 2, Bank of England: 114–129.

Butler, J. (1997). *The psychic life of power: Theories in subjection*. London: Routledge.

Camp One. (2017). *The calling of an engineer*. Available at: https://www.camp1.ca/wordpress/?page_id=2

Cassematis, P. G., & Wortley, R. (2013). Prediction of whistleblowing or non-reporting observation: The role of personal and situational factors. *Journal of Business Ethics, 117*, 615–634.

Cebr. (2016). *Engineering and economic growth: A global view.* A report for the Royal Academy of Engineering. Cebr & the Royal Academy of Engineering. Available at: http://www.raeng.org.uk/publications/reports/engineering-and-economic-growth-a-global-view.

Cohn, D. (1997). Creating crises and avoiding blame: The politics of public service reform and the new public management in Great Britain and the United States. *Administration & Society, 29*(5), 584–616.

Coleman, C. (2015). *SEC guidance supports protection for internal whistleblowing.* Available at http://www.iexology.com/library/detail.aspx?g=b72f7b2b-73eb-4563-8fc3-e2294a2fe1d2. Accessed 31 March 2017.

Contu, A. (2014) Rationality and relationality in the process of whistleblowing: Recasting whistleblowing through readings of Antigone. *Journal of Management Inquiry, 23*(4), 393–406.

Corrigan, P. W. (ed.). (2005) *On the stigma of mental illness: Practical strategies for research and social change.* Washington, DC: American Psychological Association.

Council of Europe. (2014). *Protection of whistleblowers: Recommendation CM/Rec(2014)7 and Explanatory Memorandum.* Strasbourg: Council of Europe. Available at: www.coe.int/t/dghl/standardsetting/cdcj/CDCJ%20Recommendations/CMRec(2014)7E.pdf (accessed 20 March 2017).

De Graaf, G. (2016). What works: The role of confidential integrity advisors and effective whistleblowing. *International Public Management Journal.* doi:10.1080/10967494.2015.1094163

Detert, J. R., & Burris, E. R. (2007). Leadership behaviour and employee voice: Is the door really open? *Academy of Management Journal, 50*(1), 869–884.

Devine, T. (2012). Corporate whistleblowers gain new rights and opportunities in the US. *Space for Transparency*, Transparency International, available at: http://blog.transparency.org/2012/10/01/corporate-whistleblowers-gain-new-rights-and-opportunities-in-the-us/.

Devine, T. (2015) International best practices for whistleblower statutes. In D. Lewis & W. Vandekerckhove (Eds.), *Developments in whistleblowing research 2015* (pp. 7–19). London: International Whistleblowing Research Network.

Devine, T., & Maassarani, T. (2011) *The corporate whistleblower's survival guide.* San Francisco: Berrett-Koehler.

DLA Piper. (2017). *Data protection laws of the world: United States.* Available at: https://www.dlapiperdataprotection.com/?t=law&c=US (accessed 21 January 2019).

Dondé, G. (2016). Corporate ethics policies and programmes 2016 UK and Continental Europe Survey. *Survey Ibe*, Institute of Business Ethics, available at: www.ibe.org.uk/userassets/publicationdownloads/ibe_survey_corporate_ethics_policies_and_programmes_2016_uk_and_continental_europe_survey.pdf.

Donkin, M., Smith, R., & Brown, A.J. (2008). How do officials report? Internal and external whistleblowing. In A.J. Brown (Ed.), *Whistleblowing in the Australian public sector: Enhancing the theory and practice of internal witness management in public sector organisations.* Canberra, Australia: ANU E Press.

Dutton, J. E., Ashford, S. J., O'Neill, R., Hayes, E., & Wierba, E. E. (1997). Reading the wind: How middle managers assess the context for issue selling to top managers. *Strategic Management Journal, 15*(1), 407–425.

Eberl, P., Geiger, D., & Aßländer, M. S. (2015). Repairing trust in an organization after integrity violations: The ambivalence of organizational rule adjustments. *Organization Studies, 36*(9), 1205–1235.

Engineering Council. 2010. *Engineers: An inter-country comparison: Report of a May 2010 survey of engineers in France, Germany and the UK.* Available at www.engc.org.uk/ EngCDocuments/Internet/Website/2010%20Joint%20Survey%20Report.pdf.

Engineering Council. (2015). *Guidance on whistleblowing for engineers and technicians.* Available at https://www.engc.org.uk/engcdocuments/internet/Website/Guidance%20 on%20whistleblowing.pdf (accessed 12 July 2018).

Ethics Resource Center. (2012). *Inside the mind of a whistleblower: A supplemental report of the 2011 National Business Ethics Survey.* Available at: http://www.ethics.org/nbes/ files/reportingFinal.pdf (accessed 20 March 2017).

Ethics Resource Centre (2014). *National business ethics survey.* Available at: http://www .ethics.org/nbes (accessed 9 November 2015).

EU Commission (2018). *EU Whistleblower protection.* Available at: https://ec.europa.eu/ info/law/better-regulation/initiatives/com-2018-218_en

Ewing, D. W. (1983). *Do it my way—Or you're fired! Employee rights and the changing role of management prerogatives.* New York: Wiley.

FDIC. (2013). *Bank failures in brief.* Available at https://www.fdic.gov/bank/historical/ bank/2013/index.html (accessed 25 July 2017).

Financial Conduct Authority. (2015a). *FCA introduces new rules on whistleblowing.* Available at: https://www.fca.org.uk/news/press-releases/fca-introduces-new-rules-whistleblowing.

Financial Conduct Authority. (2015b). *Whistleblowing in deposit-takers, PRA-designated investment firms and insurers.* Policy Statement PS15/24. London: Financial Conduct Authority. Available at http://fca.org.uk/your-fca/documents/policy-statements/ ps15-24 (accessed 20 March 2017).

Fish, K., Man, M., Petkov, M., & Pyman, M. (2015). *Transparency International UK Defence and Security Programme: Defence Companies Anti-Corruption Index 2015.* Transparency International UK, available at http://companies.defenceindex.org/docs/ 2015%20Defence%20Companies%20Anti-Corruption%20Index.pdf.

Fitzgerald, K. (1990). Special Report: Engineering careers: Whistle-blowing: Not always a losing game. *IEEE Spectrum,* December, 49–52.

Fotaki, M. (2014). *What market-based patient choice can't do for the NHS: The theory and evidence of how choice works in health care.* Centre for Health and the Public Interest, available at https://chpi.org.uk/wp-content/uploads/2014/03/What-market-based-patient-choice-cant-do-for-the-NHS-CHPI.pdf.

Fotaki, M. (2016). Relational ties of love – A psychosocial proposal for ethics of compassionate care in health and public services. *Psychodynamic Practice.* doi: 10.1080/ 14753634.2016.1238159.

Fotaki, M., & Humantito, I. (2015). Beyond saints and villains: Internal auditors as whistleblowers in government agencies in Indonesia. *EJ Safra Centre for Ethics blog,* May 13th. Available at http://ethics.harvard.edu/blog/beyond-saints-and-villains-internal-auditors-whistleblowers-government (accessed 20 March 2017).

Fotaki, M., Kenny, K., & Scriver, S. (2015). Whistleblowing and mental health: A new weapon for retaliation? In D. Lewis & W. Vandekerckhove (Eds.), *Developments in whistleblowing research* (pp. 106–121). London, UK: International Whistleblowing Research Network.

Foucault, M. (2001) *Fearless speech*. Los Angeles: Semiotext(e).

Foucault, M. (2005). The hermeneutics of the subject. In A. Davidson (Ed.) & G. Burchell (Trans)., *Lectures at the Collège de France, 1981–1982*. Houndmills: Palgrave Macmillan.

Foucault, M. (2010). *The government of self and others: Lectures at the Collège de France 1982–1983*. A. Davidson (Ed.) & G. Burchell (Trans). Basingstoke: Palgrave Macmillan.

Francis Public Inquiry Report. (2013). *Report on the Mid Staffordshire NHS Foundation Trust Public Inquiry*. London: The Stationery Office. Available at http://webarchive .nationalarchives.gov.uk/20150407084003/http://www.midstaffspublicinquiry.com/ report (accessed 20 March 2017).

Francis, R. (2015). *Freedom to speak up: An independent review into creating an open and honest reporting culture in the NHS*. Available at http://webarchive.nationalarchives .gov.uk/20150218150953/https://freedomtospeakup.org.uk/wp-content/uploads/2014 /07/F2SU_web.pdf.

Garside, J. (2015, November 27). HSBC whistleblower given five years' jail over biggest leak in banking history. *Guardian*, available at https://www.theguardian.com/news/ 2015/nov/27/hsbc-whistleblower-jailed-five-years-herve-falciani.

General Medical Council. (2015). *The handling by the General Medical Council of Cases involving whistleblowers. Report by the Right Honourable Sir Anthony Hooper to the General Medical Council presented on the 19th March 2015*. Available at: http://www .gmc-uk.org/Hooper_review_final_60267393.pdf (accessed 15 October 2017).

Gillespie, N., & Dietz, G. (2009). Trust repair after an organization-level failure. *Academy of Management Review, 34*(1), 127–145.

Glazer, M.P., & Glazer, P.M. (1991). *Whistleblowers: Exposing corruption in government and industry*. New York: Basic Books.

Government Accountability Project. (2012, 28 March). *BofA/Countrywide whistleblower Eileen Foster wins Ridenhour Award*. Available at https://www.whistleblower.org/ press/bofacountrywide-whistleblower-eileen-foster-wins-ridenhour-award.

Government Accountability Project. (2018, 22 February). *Press Statement: Tom Devine, Government Accountability Project Legal Director, on Digital Realty Trust, Inc. v. Somers*. Available at https://www.whistleblower.org/press/press-statement-tom-devine-government-accountability-project-legal-director-digital-realty

Grant, C. (2002). Whistleblowers: Saints of secular culture. *Journal of Business Ethics, 39*(4), 391–399.

Green, P. (2005). Disaster by design: Corruption, construction and catastrophe. *British Journal of Criminology, 45*(4), 528–546.

Greenwood, A. (2015). Whistleblowing in the Fortune 1000: What practitioners told us about wrongdoing in corporations in a pilot study. *Public Relations Review, 41*, 490–500.

Greenwood, R., & Scharfstein, D. (2013). The growth of finance. *Journal of Economic Perspectives, 27*(2), 3–28.

Gresko, J. (2018, 21 February). Supreme Court: Dodd-Frank whistleblower protection is narrow. *PBS News Hour*. Available at https://www.pbs.org/newshour/politics/supreme-court-dodd-frank-whistleblower-protection-is-narrow (accessed 14 June 2018).

Harding, L. (2014). *Snowden files: The inside story of the world's most wanted man*. London: Vintage.

Harlos, K. P. (2001). When organizational voice systems fail. More on the deaf-ear syndrome and frustration effects. *The Journal of Applied Behavioral Science, 37*(3), 324–342.

Heffernan, M. (2012). *Wilful Blindness: Why we ignore the obvious at our peril*. London: Simon & Schuster.

Hersh, M. A. (2002). Whistleblowers—heroes or traitors?: Individual and collective responsibility for ethical behaviour. *Annual Reviews in Control, 26*, 243–262.

Holtzhausen, N. (2009). Organisational trust as a prerequisite for whistleblowing. *Journal of Public Administration, 44*(1), 234–246.

House of Representatives. (2008, 23 October). *The financial crisis and the role of federal regulators: Hearings before the Committee on Oversight and Government Reform*, 110th Cong. Available at: https://www.gpo.gov/fdsys/pkg/CHRG-110hhrg55764/html/CHRG-110hhrg55764.htm

Human Rights Watch. (2015). Turkey: Mine disaster trial to open: Company officials charged, but government failures need investigation. Available at https://www.hrw.org/news/2015/04/13/turkey-mine-disaster-trial-open.

Institute of Business Ethics. (2014). Speak up. *Business Ethics Briefing 36*, available at http://www.ibe.org.uk/userassets/briefings/speak_up.pdf.

Institute of Business Ethics. (2016). Surveys on Business Ethics 2015. *Business Ethics Briefing 36*. Available at https://www.ibe.org.uk/userassets/briefings/b51_surveys2015.pdf.

Ionescu, R. (2015). Whistleblowing and disaster risk reduction. In D. Lewis & W. Vandekerckhove (Eds.), *Developments in whistleblowing research* (pp. 50–69). London: International Whistleblowing Research Network.

Jack, G. (2004). On speech, critique and protection. *Ephemera, 4*(2), 121–134.

Jackson, D., Peters, K., Andrew, S., Edenborough, M., Halcomb, E., Luck, L., . . . Wilkes, L. (2010). Trial and retribution: A qualitative study of whistleblowing and workplace relationships in nursing. *Contemporary Nurse: A Journal for the Australian Nursing Profession, 36*(1–2), 34–44.

Jagd, S. (2010). Balancing trust and control in organizations: Towards a process perspective. *Society and Business Review, 5*(3), 259–269.

Jones , C., Parker, M., & ten Bos, R. (2005). *For business ethics*. London: Routledge.

Jopson, B. (2006), Accounting for capitalism after Enron. *The Financial Times*. Available at www.ft.com/content/7592c3c6-40e6-11db-827f-0000779e2340?mhq5j=e3

Jubb, P. B. (1999). Whistleblowing: A restrictive definition and interpretation. *Journal of Business Ethics, 21*(1), 77–94.

Kaptein, M. (2011). From inaction to external whistleblowing: The influence of the ethical culture of organizations on employee responses to observed wrongdoing. *Journal of Business Ethics, 98*(3), 513–530.

Keenan, J. P. (1995). Whistleblowing and the first-level manager: Determinants of feeling obliged to blow the whistle. *Journal of Social Behavior and Personality, 10*(3), 571–584.

Kennedy, I., Howard, R., Jarman, B., & Maclean, M. (2001). *The report of the public inquiry into children's heart surgery at the Bristol Royal Infirmary 1984–1995: Learning from Bristol*. The Bristol Royal Infirmary Inquiry, available at http://webarchive.nationalarchives.gov.uk/20090811143822/http://www.bristol-inquiry.org.uk/final_report/the_report.pdf.

Kenny, K. (2014). Banking compliance and dependence corruption: Towards an attachment perspective. *Law and Financial Markets Review, 8*(2), 165–177.

Kenny, K. (2015). Constructing selves: Whistleblowing and the role of time. In D. Lewis & W. Vandekerckhove (Eds.), *Developments in whistleblowing research* (pp. 70–84). London: International Whistleblowing Research Network.

Kenny, K. (2017). Censored: Impossible speech and financial sector whistleblowers. *Human Relations.* doi:10.1177/0018726717733311.

Kenny, K. (2018, March 16). Whistleblowing systems: Common myths and how to overcome them. *Irish Times.* Available at: www.irishtimes.com/business/work/whistle blowing-systems-common-myths-and-how-to-overcome-them-1.3427102.

Kenny, K. (2019). *Whistleblowing: Towards a new theory.* Cambridge, MA: Harvard University Press.

Kenny, K. Fotaki, M., & Scriver, S. (2018). Whistleblowing and mental health: A new weapon for retaliation? *Journal of Business Ethics.* doi:10.1007/s10551-018-3868-4

Kenny, K., Fotaki, M., & Vandekerckhove, W. (2019). Whistleblowing, organization and passionate attachment. *Organisation Studies.* doi:10.1177/0170840618814558

Klaas, B. S., Olson-Buchanan, J. B., & Ward, A. (2012). The determinants of alternative forms of workplace voice: An integrative perspective. *Journal of Management, 38*(1), 314–345.

Kramer, R. M. (1999). Trust and distrust in organizations: Emerging perspectives, enduring questions. *Annual Review of Psychology, 50*(1), 569–598.

Kumagai, J. (2004). The whistle-blower's dilemma: Speaking out may be the ethical thing to do, but too often it comes at a steep price. *IEEE Spectrum.* Available at: http://spectrum.ieee.org/at-work/tech-careers/the-whistleblowers-dilemma.

Laan, A., Noorderhaven, N., Voordijk, H., & Dewulf, G. (2011). Building trust in construction partnering projects: An exploratory case-study. *Journal of Purchasing and Supply Management, 17*(2), 98–108.

Labaton Sucharow. (2012). WallStreetFleetStreetMainStreet: Corporate integrity at a crossroadsCrossroads. In *United States and United Kingdom Financial Services Industry Survey.* New York: Author.

Labaton Sucharow. (2015). *The Street, the bull, and the crisis: A survey of the US & UK financial services industry.* Available at: http://www.secwhistlebloweradvocate.com/pdf/Labaton-2015-Survey-report_12.pdf

Lane, C., & Bachmann, R. (1998). *Trust within and between organizations: Conceptual issues and empirical application.* Oxford, UK: Oxford University Press.

Langenberg, S. (2008). *Kritiek als des-organisatie. Bedrijfsethiek en waarheidspreken.* Antwerp: Garant.

Lennane, J. (1993) 'Whistleblowing': A health issue. *British Medical Journal, 307*(6905), 667–670.

Lennane, J. (1996/2012). What happens to whistleblowers, and why? *Social Medicine, 6*(4), 249–258.

Lewis, D. (2011). Whistleblowing in a changing legal climate: Is it time to revisit our approach to trust and loyalty at the workplace? *Business Ethics: A European Review, 20*(1), 71–87.

Lewis, D., D'Angelo, A., & Clarke, L. (2015). Industrial relations and the management of whistleblowing after the Francis Report: What can be learned from the evidence? *Industrial Relations Journal, 46*(4), 312–327.

Lewis, D., Brown, A. J., & Moberly, R. (2014). "Whistleblowing, its importance and the state of the research. In A. J. Brown, R. Motherly, D. Lewis, & W. Vandekerckhove

(Eds.), *International handbook on whistleblowing research*. Cheltenham: Edward Elgar.

Lewis, D., & Vandekerckhove, W. (2015). Does following a whistleblowing procedure make a difference? The evidence from the research conducted for The Francis Inquiry. In D. Lewis & W. Vandekerckhove (Eds.), *Developments in whistleblowing research* (pp. 85–105). London: International Whistleblowing Research Network.

Lewis, D., & Vandekerckhove, W. (2018). Trade unions and the whistleblowing process in the UK: An opportunity for strategic expansion? *Journal of Business Ethics, 148*(4), 835–845.

Liang, J., Farh, C. J., & Farh, J. L. (2012). Psychological antecedents of promotive and prohibitive voice: A two-wave examination. *Academy of Management Journal, 55,* 71–92.

Lovell, A. (2002). Ethics as a dependent variable in individual and organisational decision making. *Journal of Business Ethics, 37*(2), 145–163.

Loyens, K., & Maesschalck, J. (2014). Whistleblowing and power. In A. J. Brown, D. Lewis, R. Moberly, & W. Vandekerckhove (Eds.), *The international whistleblowing research handbook* (pp. 154–175). Cheltenham: Edward Elgar.

Mansbach, A. (2009). Keeping democracy vibrant: Whistleblowing as truth-telling in the workplace. *Constellations: An International Journal of Critical and Democratic Theory, 16*(3), 363–376.

Mansbach, A. (2011). Whistleblowing as fearless speech: The radical democratic effects of late modern parrhesia. In D. Lewis & W. Vandekerckhove (Eds.), *Whistleblowing and democratic values*. Available at https www.academia.edu/1348441/Whistleblowing_and_Democratic Values. Accessed 20 September 2016.

Marks, S. (2016). The silent man of LuxLeaks fights back. *Politico*, available at: http://www.politico.eu/article/silent-man-of-luxleaks-fights-back-raphael-halet/.

Martin, B. and Rifkin, W. (2004). The dynamics of employee dissent: Whistleblowers and organizational Jiu-Jitsu. *Public Organization Review: A Global Journal 4,* 221–238.

Martin, D. (2012, February 4). Roger Boisjoly, 73, dies; warned of shuttle danger. *New York Times*, available at: http://www.nytimes.com/2012/02/04/us/roger-boisjoly-73-dies-warned-of-shuttle-danger.html

Maynes, T. D., & Podsakoff, P. M. (2014). Speaking more broadly: An examination of the nature, antecedents, and consequences of an expanded set of employee voice behaviors. *Journal of Applied Psychology, 34,* 112–123.

Mellors-Bourne, R., May, T., Haynes, K., & Talbot, M. (2017). Engineering UK 2017: The state of engineering. *Engineering UK*, available at: http://www.engineeringuk.com/media/1355/enguk-report-2017.pdf

McEvily, B. (2011). Reorganizing the boundaries of trust: From discrete alternatives to hybrid forms. *Organization Science, 22*(5), 1266–1276.

Mesmer-Magnus, J., & Visveswaran, C. (2005). Whistleblowing in organizations: An examination of correlates of whistleblowing intentions, actions, and retaliation. *Journal of Business Ethics, 62*(3), 277–297.

Miceli, M. P., & Near, J. P. (1992). *Blowing the whistle: The organizational and legal implications for companies and employees*. New York: Lexington Books.

Miceli, M. P., Near, J. P., & Dworkin, T. M. (2008). *Whistleblowing in organizations*. New York: Routledge.

Miethe, T. D. (1999). *Whistleblowing at work: Tough choices in exposing fraud, waste, and abuse on the job*. Boulder: Westview.

Miles, M., & Huberman, A. (1994). *An expanded sourcebook: Qualitative data analysis*. Thousand Oaks, CA: Sage.

Milliken, F. J., Morrison, E. W., & Hewlin, P. F. (2003). An exploratory study of employee silence: Issues that employees don't communicate upward and why. *Journal of Management Studies, 40*(6), 1453–1476.

Moberly, R., & Wylie, L. E. (2011). An empirical study of whistleblower policies in United States corporate codes of ethics. In D. Lewis & W. Vandekerckhove (Eds.), *Whistleblowing and democratic values* (pp. 27–55). London: International Whistleblowing Research Network.

Möllering, G. (2001). The nature of trust: From Georg Simmel to a theory of expectation, interpretation and suspension. *Sociology, 35*(2), 403–420.

Möllering, G. (2006). *Trust: Reason, routine, reflexivity*. Oxford: Elsevier.

Möllering, G. (2013). Process views of trusting and crises. In R. Bachmann & A. Zaheer (Eds.), *Handbook of advances in trust research* (pp. 285–305). Cheltenham: Edward Elgar.

Morrison, E. W. (2011). Employee voice behavior: Integration and directions for future research. *Academy of Management Annals, 5*, 373–412.

Morrison, E. W., & Milliken, F. J. (2000). Organizational silence: A barrier to change and development in a pluralistic world. *Academy of Management review, 25*(4), 706–725.

Mowbray, P. K., Wilkinson, A., & Tse, H. H. M. (2015). An integrative review of employee voice: Identifying a common conceptualization and research agenda. *International Journal of Management Reviews, 17*, 382–400.

Near, J. P., & Miceli, M. P. (1985). Organizational dissidence: The case of whistleblowing. *Journal of Business Ethics, 4*(1), 1–16.

Near, J. P., Dworkin, T. M., & Miceli, M. P. (1993). Explaining the whistle-blowing process: Suggestions from power theory and justice theory. *Organization Science, 4*(3), 393–411.

Nooteboom, B. (1996). Trust, opportunism and governance: A process and control model. *Organization Studies, 17*(6), 985–1010.

Nooteboom, B. (2006). *Forms, sources and processes of trust*. CentER Discussion Paper; Vol. 2006-40.

Nyberg, P. (2011). *Misjudging risks: The causes of the systemic banking crisis in Ireland*. Report available at http://www.bankinginquiry.gov.ie (accessed 14 April 2012).

O'Grady, S. (2010). Credit crisis cost the nation £7.4trillion, says Bank of England. *The Independent*, available at http://www.independent.co.uk/news/business/news/credit-crisis-cost-the-nation-1637trn-says-bank-of-england-1931569.html

O'Brien, J. (2003). *Wall Street on trial: A corrupted state?* Chichester: Wiley.

Odell, R. A. (2013). Caltrans hit with $570,000 verdict for whistleblower retaliation. *Orange County Employment Attorney Blog*, available at http://orangecountyemploymentattorneyblog.com/caltrans-hit-570000-verdict-whistleblower-retaliation/

OECD. (2011). *G20 anti-corruption action plan protection of whistleblowers*. Available at https://www.oecd.org/g20/topics/anti-corruption/48972967.pdf (accessed 14 June 2018).

Oliver, D. (2003). Whistle-blowing engineer. *Journal of Professional Issues in Engineering Education and Practice, 129*(4), 246–256.

OSHA. (2018). Whistleblower Investigation Data. Available at: https://www.whistleblowers
.gov/sites/default/files/3DCharts-FY2007-FY2017.pdf (accessed 20 June 2018).

Parmerlee, M. A., Near, J. P., & Jensen, T. C. (1982). Correlates of whistleblowers' perceptions of organizational reprisals. *Administrative Science Quarterly, 27*(1), 17–34.

Partnoy, F. (2006). A revisionist view of Enron and the sudden death of 'May'. In P. H.
Dembinski, C. Lager, Cornford, A., & Bonvin, J.-M. (Eds.), *Enron and world finance:
A case study in ethics* (pp. 57–89). New York: Palgrave Macmillan & Observatoire de
la Finance.

PCAW. (2016). *Whistleblowing, time for change.* London: Public Concern at Work.
Available at https://s3-eu-west-1.amazonaws.com/public-concern-at-work/wp-content/
uploads/images/2018/09/08221332/PCAW_5yr-review_Time-for-a-Change.pdf

Peters, K., Luck, L., Hutchinson, M., Wilkes, L., Andrew, S., & Jackson, D. (2011). The
emotional sequelae of whistleblowing: Findings from a qualitative study. *Journal of
Clinical Nursing, 20*(19–20), 2907–2914.

Petersen, J. C., & Farrell, D. (1986). *Whistleblowing: Ethical and legal issues in expressing
dissent.* Dubuque, IA: Kendall/Hunt.

Pohler, D. M., & Luchak, A. A. (2014). The missing employee in employee voice research.
In A. Wilkinson, J. Donaghey, T. Dundon, & R. Freeman (Eds.), *The handbook of
research on employee voice* (pp. 188–207). Cheltenham: Elgar Press.

Premeaux, S., & Bedeian, A. (2003). Breaking the silence: The moderating effects of
self-monitoring in predicting speaking up in the workplace. *Journal of Management
Studies, 40*, 1537–1562.

Public Concern at Work. (2013.) *Silence in the city.* Available at http://www.pcaw.org.uk/
silence-in-the-city-whistleblowing-in-financial-services (accessed 15 October 2017).

Public Concern at Work. (2013). *Silence in the city: Whistleblowing in the financial services.* Available at http://www.pcaw.org.uk/law-policy/whistleblowing-commission/
silence-in-the-city-whistleblowing-in-financial-services.

Public Concern at Work. (2014). *Code of practice.* London: Public Concern at Work.

Public Concern at Work. (2016). *Whistleblowing: Time for change releases five year review.*
Available at http://www.pcaw.org.uk/content/6-campaigns/2-time-for-change-review/
pcaw_5yr-review_final.pdf?1480418791

Rankin, J. (2018). EU moves to bring in whistleblower protection law. *The Guardian,*
16 April. Available at https://www.theguardian.com/world/2018/apr/16/eu-moves-to-
bring-in-whistleblower-protection-law-yax-avoidance-emissions-scandals (accessed
14 June 2018).

Rehg, M. T., Miceli, M. P., Near, J. P., & Van Scotter, J. R. (2008). Antecedents and
outcomes of retaliation against whistleblowers: Gender differences and power relationships. *Organization Science, 19*(2), 221–240.

Roberts, P., Brown, A. J., & Olsen, J. (2011). *Whistling while they work: A good-practice
guide for managing internal reporting of wrongdoing in public sector organisations.*
Australia: ANU E Press.

Robinson, D. (2015). 'I am not a martyr', says LuxLeaks whistleblower facing jail. *Financial Times*, available at: https://www.ft.com/content/110e2524-b925-11e4-a8d0-0014
4feab7de

Rothschild, J. (2013). The fate of whistleblowers in nonprofit organizations. *Nonprofit and
Voluntary Sector Quarterly, 42*(5), 886–901.

Rothschild, J., & Miethe, T. D. (1999). Whistle-blower disclosures and management retaliation. *Work and Occupations, 26*(1), 107–128.

Saunders, M., Dietz, G., & Thornhill, A. (2014). Trust and distrust: Polar opposites or independent but co-existing? *Human Relations, 67*(6), 639–665.

Sherman, M. (2009). *A short history of financial deregulation in the United States.* Washington, DC: Center for Economic and Policy Research, available at http://cepr.net/documents/publications/dereg-timeline-2009-07.pdf

Skivenes, M., & Trygstad, S. (2010). When whistle-blowing works: The Norwegian case. *Human Relations, 63*(7), 1071–1097.

Sims, R. L., & Keenan, J. P. (1998). Predictors of external whistleblowing: Organizational and intrapersonal variables. *Journal of Business Ethics, 17*(4), 411–421.

Smith, R., & Brown, A. J. (2008). The good, the bad and the ugly: Whistleblowing outcomes. In *Whistleblowing in the Australian public sector: Enhancing the theory and practice of internal witness management in public sector organizations* (pp. 129–134). Canberra: ANU epress.

Stansbury, N., & Stansbury, C. (2010). Engineers against corruption: Preventing corruption in the infrastructure sector – What can engineers do?, in *Engineering: Issues, challenges and opportunities for development.* Paris: UNESCO Publishing.

Stothard, M., & Buck, T. (2015). HSBC tax leaker to advise Spain's Podemos party. *Financial Times,* available at: https://www.ft.com/content/bc6d9ffc-b070-11e4-a2cc-00144feab7de.

Strauss, A., & Corbin, J. (1990). *Basics of qualitative research.* London: Sage.

Tenbrunsel, A., & Thomas, J. (2015). *The Street, the bull and the crisis: A survey of the US & UK financial services industry.* The University of Notre Dame and Labaton Sucharow LLP, available at https://www.secwhistlebloweradvocate.com/pdf/Labaton-2015-Survey-report_12.pdf

The Telegraph. (2001). History of scandal. Available at www.telegraph.co.uk/news/1334437/History-of-scandal.html

Thomas, P.G. (2005). Debating a whistle-blower protection act for employees of the government of Canada. *Canadian Public Administration, 48*(2), 147–184.

Timmermans, S., & Tavory, I. (2012). Theory construction in qualitative research: From grounded theory to abductive analysis. *Sociological Theory, 30*(3), 167–186.

Ting, A. (2014). Luxembourg leaks: How harmful tax competition leads to profit shifting. *Conversation.* Available at https://theconversation.com/luxembourg-leaks-how-harmful-tax-competition-leads-to-profit-shifting-33940

Transparency International Ireland. (2017). *Speak up report 2017.* Transparency International Ireland: Dublin. Available at https://www.transparency.ie/sites/default/files/17.12.13_speak_up_report_ie_final.pdf Access date: 12 July 2018

U.S. Securities and Exchange Commission. (2013). 2013 *Annual Report to Congress on the Dodd-Frank Whistleblower Program.* Available at https://www.sec.gov/files/annual-report-2013.pdf

U.S. Securities and Exchange Commission. (2014). *2014 Annual Report to Congress on the Dodd-Frank Whistleblower Program.* Available at https://www.sec.gov/about/offices/owb/annual-report-2014.pdf

Uys, T. 2008. Rational loyalty and whistleblowing: The South African context. *Current Sociology, 56*(6), 904–921.

van der Velden, P. G., Pecoraro, M., Houwerzijl, M. S., & van der Meulen, E. (2018). Mental health problems among whistleblowers: A comparative study. *Psychological Reports*, 1–13.

Vandekerckhove, W. (2006). *Whistleblowing and organizational social responsibility: A global assessment*. Aldershot: Ashgate.

Vandekerckhove, W. (2010). European whistleblowing policies: Tiers or tears? In D. B. Lewis (Ed.), *A global approach to public interest disclosure* (pp. 15–35). Cheltenham: Edward Elgar.

Vandekerckhove, W. (2013). *Providing an alternative to silence: Towards greater protection and support for whistleblowers in Belgium*. Brussels: Transparency International Belgium.

Vandekerckhove, W., & Commers, M. R. (2004). Whistle blowing and rational loyalty. *Journal of Business Ethics, 53*(1–2), 225–233.

Vandekerckhove, W. & Phillips, A. (2017). Whistleblowing as a protracted process: A study of UK whistleblower journeys. *Journal of Business Ethics*. doi:10.1007/s10551-017-3727-8.

Vandekerckhove, W., & Rumyantseva, N. (2014). *Freedom to speak up: Qualitative research report*. London: University of Greenwich.

Vandekerckhove, W., & Langenberg, S. (2012). Can we organize courage? Implications of Foucault's parrhesia. *Electronic Journal of Business Ethics and Organisation Studies, 17*(2), 35–44.

Vandekerckhove, W., & Lewis, D. (2012). The content of whistleblowing procedures: A critical review of recent official guidelines *Journal of Business Ethics, 108*(2), 253–564.

Vandekerckhove, W., Brown, A. J., & Tsahuridu, E. E. (2014). Managerial responses to whistleblowing. In A. J. Brown, D. Lewis, R. Moberly, & W. Vandekerckhove (Eds.), *International handbook on whistleblowing research* (pp. 298–327). Cheltenham: Edward Elgar.

Vandekerckhove, W., Fotaki, M., Kenny, K., & Humantito, I. (2016). Speak-up arrangements as processes of trusting in organizations. 32nd EGOS Colloquium, Naples.

Vandekerckhove, W., Fotaki, M., Kenny, K., Humantito, I. J., & Ozdemir Kaya, D. (2016). *Effective speak-up arrangements for whistle-blowers: A multi-case study on the role of responsiveness, trust and culture*. ACCA & ESRC. Available at http://www.accaglobal.com/content/dam/acca/global/PDF-technical/corporate-governance/ACCA-ESRC%20Effective%20Speak-Up%20Arrangements%20for%20Whistle-Blowers%20-%20Recommendations%20for%20Managers.pdf

Vandekerckhove, W., James, C., & West, F. (2013). *Whistleblowing: The inside story—a study of the experiences of 1,000 whistleblowers*. London: Public Concern at Work.

van Steenbergen, R. (2014, *8 August*). Developments in whistleblowing protection in the Netherlands. Huis Voor Klokkenluiders. Available at: https://huisvoorklokkenluiders.nl/wp-content/uploads/2015/03/Developments-in-whistleblowing-protection-in-the-Netherlands.pdf

Véron, N., Autret, M., & Galichon, A. (2004). *L'information financière en crise: comptabilité et capitalisme*. Odile Jacob: Paris.

Waldron, N. (2012). *The effectiveness of hotlines in detecting and deterring malpractice in organisations*. London: Institute of Business Ethics.

Watzlawick, P., Beavin-Bavelas, J., & Jackson, D. (1967.) Some tentative axioms of communication. *In* Pragmatics of human communication: A study of interactional patterns, pathologies and paradoxes. New York: W. W. Norton.

Wayne, L., Carr, K., Guevara, M. W., Cabra, M., & Hudson, M. (2014). Leaked documents expose global companies' secret tax deals in Luxembourg. *International Consortium of Investigative Journalists*, available at https://www.icij.org/project/luxembourg-leaks/leaked-documents-expose-global-companies-secret-tax-deals-luxembourg.

Weber, J., & Wasieleski, D. M. (2013). Corporate ethics and compliance programs: A report, analysis and critique *Journal of Business Ethics, 112*(4), 609–626.

Weiskopf, R., & Tobias-Miersch. (2016). Whistleblowing, parrhesia and the contestation of truth in the workplace. *Organisation Studies, 37*(11), 1621–1640.

Weiskopf, R., & Willmott, H. (2013). Ethics as critical practice: The 'Pentagon Papers', deciding responsibly, truth-telling, and the unsettling of organizational morality. *Organization Studies, 34*(4), 469–493.

Whistleblowing International Network. (2016). *Win statement on Luxleaks trial verdict.* Available at https://www.pcaw.org.uk/latest/blog/win-statement-on-luxleaks-trial-verdict

Wilcutt, T., & Whitmeyer, T. (2013). The case for safety: The North Sea Piper Alpha disaster. *Nasa Safety Center System Failure Case Study, 7*(4), 1–4, National Aeronautics and Space Administration (NASA), available at https://nsc.nasa.gov/SFCS/SystemFailureCaseStudy/Details/112

Worth, M. (2013). *Whistleblowing in Europe: Legal protections for whistleblowers in the EU.* Transparency International. Available at http://www.transparency.org/whatwedo/publication/whistleblowing_in_europe_legal_protections_for_whistleblowers_in_the_eu (accessed 15 October 2017).

Speak-up Arrangements – Key Theories

We found several theories to be crucial in informing our work on speak-up arrangements. They are summarized here briefly for reference. Each is part of an ongoing research agenda and is therefore changing and evolving over time, so this summary is incomplete, but hopefully gives a good indication of the background. We link these theories together, and by doing so build upon each. By supplementing this with the analysis of our empirical work we culminate with our proposed framework for understanding and implementing speak up arrangements.

EMPLOYEE VOICE

We start our framework with employee voice, because whistleblowing is an act of employees using their voice in their organizations to speak up about wrongdoing. Employee voice is more of a research stream than a theory, but this area of inquiry has important implications for whistleblowing studies. There are three general streams in the area of employee voice: the organizational behavior (OB) stream, the human resource management (HRM) stream and the employee relations (ER) stream. HRM/ER scholars tend to see voice as a way in which employees influence work practices and decisions either directly or indirectly through collective representation, and OB tends to see voice as a matter of individual workers communicating information for the benefit of the organization. The divergence in streams has led some researchers to try to synthesize the two views, which is done by moving away from the focus on motivation for speaking out, and instead acknowledging that it happens, and focusing on how to deal with it when it does.[1] This synthesis had informed research on whistleblowing as well as recent legislation by downplaying the motivation for speaking up. Indeed in many whistleblower protection laws, motivation is not a factor that impacts upon whether a whistleblower is protected or not.

FEARLESS SPEECH—FOUCAULT 2001, 2010

Whistleblowing is more than employee voice, however. Whistleblowers suffer, and so they speak up at some risk to themselves. This notion of risk led us to theories of Parrhesia. Parrhesia is a concept from Ancient Greece that is used and developed in the work of Michel Foucault. It is a type of speech that is bold, shocking and truthful, and was used in political discussions in Ancient Greece to oppose the rhetoric that pervaded political life. The key points of fearless speech are as follows:

1. It is a necessary condition for democracy: 'Frankly speaking truth' is a necessity and is elicited by the dynamic of the agora.
2. It is done by someone who is inferior to those for whom the critical and morally motivated truth is intended.
3. It is a democratic right: as a citizen of Athens, citizens had the right and some even had a moral obligation to use parrhesia.
4. It is a necessary condition for care because caring for the self as a matter of telling yourself the truth is presupposed in order to be able to take care of others, of the polis.
5. It implies both having and displaying courage, because speaking truth in public presupposes the courage to contradict the prevailing discourse, the public, the sovereign. This could mean that the parrhesiastes might risk his/her life.
6. It presupposes self-critique as a precondition for a moral attitude.

This speaking truth to power at serious risk to oneself, is a useful framing for the whistleblowing process, and highlights the importance of the recipient. It provides theoretical justification for creating and implementing speak-up arrangements. However, organizations that institutionalize whistleblowing through the introduction of speak-up systems and whistleblowing hotlines run the risk of deadening parrhesiastic critique, because they systemize a process that needs to contain an element of spontaneity and surprise in order to be truly interruptive. (See also Kenny et al., 2019.)

TRUST—MÖLLERING 2013

When using fearless speech, there needs to be some trust that the speech will be heard, even if there are still risks to the whistleblower. Theories of trust are key to both whistleblowing research and to understanding the challenges and best practices of speak-up arrangements. There are multiple theories of trust, but in this book we draw on the theory developed by Möllering. This view frames trust as a mental process that encompasses the elements of expectation, interpretation, and suspension. So in the context of whistleblowing, a trusting whistleblower expects their speak-up to be taken seriously and acted upon, they interpret the feedback that they get from managements and the speak-up operator, and any uncertainty is overlooked and replaced with a 'leap of faith' that the outcome will be satisfactory. An untrusting whistleblower will not be able to make the leap of faith. Thus, past experiences, present interpretations and a sense of hope influence whether trust is present or not. In addition, Möllering emphasizes that trusting is not only formative for individual identity but also for collective identity: 'trusting signals and confirms an actor's willingness to belong to a collective' (p. 294). Speak-up arrangements both stimulate trust in the organization if they are implemented and operated well, but they also require trust to be effective. For example, in our study, interviewees were of the view that employees normally raise a concern about wrongdoing with their line manager, and only use a speak-up channel when there is a lack of trust between the employee and this person. In this way the speak-up arrangement fosters trust that is otherwise lacking. However, the arrangement needs to be trusted as well, if the organization fails to convey an expectation to the whistleblower that he or she will be taken seriously and treated well—for instance, by providing and sharing cases of successful whistleblowing. This could lead to the whistleblower not trusting the speak-up arrangement and turning to an external recipient instead (see also Vandekerckhove, James, and West, 2013).

ETHICAL CULTURE—KAPTEIN 2011

Employees using their voices to engage in fearless speech and trusting that the hearer will listen and act on what they say contributes to an ethical culture in the workplace. Muel Kaptein has developed the Corporate Ethical Virtue Model that helps us understand ethical culture more clearly. He identifies seven virtues that stimulate organization members to behave in an ethical manner. The virtues identified are clarity, congruency, feasibility, supportability, transparency, discussability and sanctionability. Kaptein hypothesized how the presence of each virtue would affect the likelihood that an employee would speak up using various channels; whether they would remain silent, confront the wrongdoer, raise it with a manager, call the hotline or go to an external recipient. He found that various virtues had different impacts, but did not test the combination of virtues, or how the influence changes with additional speak-ups. His research is helpful, however, in understanding how the culture of an organization influences how individuals will speak up, and aids in showing how speak-up arrangements can be tailored to specific cultures. To be successful, they must be not only written in the language that people can understand but also must take account of organizational cultures (for example, has there already been negative publicity around whistleblowers in the organization?) and different sectors (what legal requirements are there to speak up and how does the speak-up arrangement compliment these?) as well as national cultures (in Japan, for instance where employees often have jobs for life, how does the permanence of their employment affect how they can speak up?). This is particularly important when setting up speaking up arrangements in global company through its local subsidiaries.

INTERACTIONAL COMMUNICATION—WATZLAWICK ET AL. 1967

The Interactional Communication theory has five axioms, two of which are helpful in a whistleblowing context. The first of Watzlawick's axioms that we draw upon states that every communication consists of a 'content' and a 'relationship' aspect. When a worker is saying something is going wrong in the organization, they are informing someone about the wrongdoing. That is the content aspect of their communication: some facts and their evaluation of these facts as wrongdoing. There is also a relationship aspect of that communication—namely, they are also communicating that they are not able to prevent or stop that wrongdoing. This indicates that they cannot stop it themselves and therefore are seeking help from another. This relationship aspect allows for interpretation of the content. Hence it is a communication about the communication, or a meta-communication. Since the relationship aspect of whistleblowing is a communication from someone who does not have power to someone who has power (or is assumed to have power), the meta-communication comes down to 'you do something about this wrongdoing'. For example, in the *Challenger* space shuttle disaster, Roger Boisjoly and other engineers at Thiolkol Inc. tried to convince their managers to intervene in the launch. In doing so, they communicated that they were not able to stop the launch, and expected that their managers could.

The second axiom of Watzlawick's communication theory we use is that 'one cannot not communicate'. In a whistleblowing context, this means that a recipient cannot not respond. No response is seen by the whistleblower as a very clear response—namely that the recipient doesn't care. Both of these axioms point to the importance of a recipient responding to speak-ups in an appropriate way and visibly responding to the individual who raises it. Although there are challenges to doing this effectively, the theory highlights the needs to react appropriately. For example, in the bank in our study, an anonymous report was sent to HR. Although HR investigated and found nothing wrong, because the response was invisible, the reporting employee thought that nothing was being done. This 'nonresponse' signaled to the employee that the concern was not being taken seriously and she escalated it to outside recipients. In this case the 'nonresponse' (invisible response) was taken as a very clear sign that the issue was not important.

ENDNOTE

1. Mowbray et al. (2015).

Project Methodology

SAMPLE AND DATA COLLECTION

Our focus was on internal whistleblowing recipients because of a lack of research into this group, and our initial assumptions that this would offer valuable insights. We collected primary date in the form of interviews with 23 internal whistleblowing recipients in four organizations and seven external recipients and advisors ($n = 30$). The first group: recipients of internal whistleblowing claims held positions ranging from: compliance officer, HR manager, HR director, legal counsel, investigator and auditor. The organizations comprised a UK National Health Service Trust, an engineering multinational, a bank with offices in Western Europe and the United States and a central government agency in Southeast Asia. In addition to interview material, we requested and were provided with documents including annual reports, whistleblowing policies, and intranet screenshots. In addition, we interviewed a range of external recipients of disclosures including: a speak-up consultant, a hotline operator, an external ombudsman, an independent advice line operator, a law-firm partner and two regulators. The primary interviews were conducted both in person and where necessary via telephone, between November 2015 and February 2016. Each lasted between 40 and 90 minutes. Interview schedules encompassed questions on how the organization had designed, implemented, communicated and managed their internal speak-up arrangements. We were also interested in people's experiences: the successes they had had and the challenges they experienced. Our questions also focused on how processes were operated in practice but also whether and how these processes enabled whistleblowers' concerns to be taken further. Each interview was recorded and then transcribed verbatim before checking for accuracy.

ANALYSIS

Our analysis proceeded via an abductive strategy, which enables unusual and surprising findings to emerge, and the development of theories in response to this.[1] Abductive analysis considers that, unlike grounded theory, a-priori conceptual frameworks are both present and influential in the analysis of new empirical data. The focus is upon iteration between consideration of data, in-depth and further reading of relevant theoretical approaches, to develop new frameworks and insights (Timmermans and Tavory, 2012). For Timmermans and Tavory (2012: 176) such iterations allow 'a theoretically salient image' to emerge in relation to a particular concept, one 'that illuminates different aspects of the data and fore-grounds previously undistinguishable facets.' For example, in this case where the authors were working on theories relating to ethics, transparency, organizational culture and context, and trust. Analysis thus proceeded through members of the team, who had not been involved in a particular case, developing initial codes 'within case'.[2] Next, we drew on strategies for cross-case comparison[3] in order to connect common threads between themes. Again we followed an iterative process with each author separately considering the emergent themes to date before coming together to discuss. Qualitative data analysis software was used in order to organize the emergent themes and categories. From an initial set of 120 codes, eight main themes arose around: 'trust', 'lack of trust', 'communication', 'power', 'emotions', 'reasons for not using speak-up procedure', 'reasons for using speak-up procedure'. We then worked up these themes in many cases in conjunction with interviewees and practitioners, presenting ongoing research at industry events (Vandkerckhove et al., 2016a),[4] incorporating feedback into the ongoing development of our analysis.

ENDNOTES

1. Timmermans and Tavory (2012).
2. Strauss and Corbin (1998).
3. Miles and Huberman (1994).
4. Vandkerckhove et al. (2016a).

Other Resources

TEACHING AND LEARNING RESOURCES

We have developed a number of useful resources to accompany this book. These include a module outline with a session-by-session teaching overview of the key issues set out, learning outcomes, a full reading list and information on relevant journal publications. A set of PowerPoint lecture notes is available alongside this. The website www.clipsaboutwork.org provides useful teaching video clips for key issues raised in this book and in the proposed lecture sessions. Finally, we have developed nine teaching case studies, and each can be used alone or alongside our proposed module outline. These help to bring students' awareness to 'real life' situations, and develop analytic capabilities around the key topics we address.

ONLINE RESOURCES

Various resources are available that can be used in conjunction with this book. One such resource is **Whistleblowing Impact** (www.whistleblowingimpact.org) a website on whistleblowing that has been developed by academic researchers (including the authors) who wish to make their findings available to a wider audience outside the university. The website offers practical guides informed by research on a number of topics including: the financial cost of whistleblowing, postdisclosure career survival strategies for whistleblowers, the impacts of speaking out, and whistleblowing in sectors including health and financial services. The website features videos, downloads and podcasts that help put the research into context. Links are provided to other related research and to key whistleblower support organizations.

Of particular relevance to this book is the material on *Effective Speak-up Arrangements*. This section provides an overview of this research, some of which is referenced in Chapter 3 of this book. It also includes three short videos:

1. An accessible cartoon-based overview of the main issues.
2. An interview with one of the authors in which he discusses how the research was conducted and the main findings.

3. A video from the launch of the report that was written for the Association of Chartered Certified Accountants (ACCA), in which findings are presented and a panel discussion takes place.

These can help the reader to understand how the research was generated from real organizations with real issues, and to learn how the issues discussed affect a broad range of companies. Additionally, there are guides and recommendations for how managers and directors can play a part in ensuring that speak-up arrangements are the best they can be.

Other resources are available from various NGOs:

Transparency International is an anticorruption NGO that has branches in over 100 countries. Several of these countries are involved in work on whistleblower protection as a priority. They publish reports, survey results and other resources. The Irish chapter for example provides an Integrity Network for businesses that offers advice on whistleblowing procedures, a helpline and guides for speaking up safely. It also provides regular and up-to-date surveys on whistleblowing attitudes within wider society:

https://www.transparency.org/
http://transparency.eu/
http://transparency.ie/
http://transparency.org.au/

Public Concern at Work is the Whistleblowing Charity in the UK. It operates an advice line that individuals can call into to get advice on how to make a disclosure, or what protections are available to them if they have already spoken up. PCAW also works with businesses to design and implement speak-up arrangements, and publishes practical reports and case studies based on this work:

http://www.pcaw.org.uk/

The Government Accountability Project in the United States is a whistleblower protection and advocacy organization. It is a nonpartisan public-interest group that litigates whistleblower cases, helps expose wrongdoing to the public, and actively promotes government and corporate accountability:

https://www.whistleblower.org/

Index